FINANCIAL
Mastery
for the Career Teacher

FINANCIAL
Mastery
for the Career Teacher

GENE SICILIANO

CORWIN
A SAGE Company

For information:

Corwin
A SAGE Company
2455 Teller Road
Thousand Oaks, California 91320
(800) 233-9936
Fax: (800) 417-2466
www.corwin.com

SAGE India Pvt. Ltd.
B 1/I 1 Mohan Cooperative
   Industrial Area
Mathura Road, New Delhi 110 044
India

SAGE Ltd.
1 Oliver's Yard
55 City Road
London EC1Y 1SP
United Kingdom

SAGE Asia-Pacific Pte. Ltd.
33 Pekin Street #02-01
Far East Square
Singapore 048763

Library of Congress Cataloging-in-Publication Data

Siciliano, Gene.
Financial mastery for the career teacher/Gene Siciliano.
      p. cm.
Includes bibliographical references and index.
ISBN 978-1-4129-7500-1 (pbk.)
   1. Teachers—Finance, Personal. 2. First-year teachers—Finance, Personal. I. Title.

HG179.S469 2010
332.0240024'3711—dc22   2009051377

This book is printed on acid-free paper.

10   11   12   13   14   10   9   8   7   6   5   4   3   2   1

Acquisitions Editor:	Hudson Perigo
Associate Editor:	Julie McNall
Editorial Assistant:	Allison Scott
Production Editor:	Cassandra Margaret Seibel
Copy Editor:	Pam Schroeder
Typesetter:	C&M Digitals (P) Ltd.
Proofreader:	Sarah J. Duffy
Indexer:	Jean Casalegno
Cover Designer:	Rose Storey

Contents

**Interactive Financial Planning
Tools Available Online**

Additional materials and resources related to
Financial Mastery for the Career Teacher can be
found at http://www.corwin.com/financialmastery

Acknowledgments

When I wrote my first book in 2003, *Finance for Non-Financial Managers*, I remember how difficult I thought it would be to put my ideas into writing and have them actually look like something that would be in print forever (with luck). It turns out I had the entire book in my head, and I was able to write every word without reference to any outside sources in about 6 months. I don't think there was a single footnote reference in the entire book. My second book was a manual that was so lean, at the request of the publisher, that it never got beyond one printing. It currently exists as a rarely sought-after e-book.

This book is different. It has very different content for a very different audience—the individual teacher, instructor, or professor—the very important people who teach our kids but who are not involved in a profit-making enterprise. IRAs (individual retirement accounts) are more important than stock offerings, and college for the kids trumps interest in cost accounting by a wide margin. The research for this book, including the newest programs for employee benefits and legislation for credit cards, was mostly done online, a new experience for me. There is so much information available on the Internet that I didn't make a single trip to the library.

I did, however, have the support and assistance of some good friends and advisers who helped make this book possible. I must first thank my editor, Hudson Perigo, who convinced me to write this book in the first place. She had a clear vision of its value to the profession that Corwin serves, and I'm grateful for the confidence she placed in me to write it. My thanks also to Daniel Feiman, Ivan Rosenberg, and Lee Schwartz, all seasoned consultants and experts in their own fields, for reading some of the manuscript and providing insights into things I missed, misstated, or just misspelled. I'm particularly grateful to Daniel Feiman, who helped me improve the online tools that were created to accompany the book.

And once again, I was blessed with the unwavering support of my beloved partner, Karen Dellosso, who let me work still later than usual on this, tolerated my grumbling when it didn't go well, and let me slip out of town for a couple of critical weeks to focus on the writing.

To all of you, my sincere thanks.

Publisher's Acknowledgments

Corwin gratefully acknowledges the contributions of the following reviewers:

Sheri Fisher
Teacher
Ceres, CA

Richard Sarmiento
Sixth-Grade Teacher
Taylor Elementary School
Stockton, CA

Jaime Schulze
Social Science Teacher
Fresno, CA

About the Author

**Gene Siciliano**, CMC, CPA, is a financial management consultant. His business is helping companies to manage their businesses more profitably. His tools of the trade include management advisory services, business planning and modeling, financial department effectiveness audits, board service, management coaching, and a series of training and workshop programs, largely focused on finance and accounting for predominantly nonfinancial clients.

A longtime member of the National Speakers Association and an avid communicator, Mr. Siciliano speaks to corporate and association audiences nationwide on financial and management topics. His articles on financial management, business planning, and cost control have been published internationally. He also publishes both print and electronic newsletters on financial management topics, as well as a blog.

Following graduation from Penn State University's Smeal College with a business degree in accounting, Mr. Siciliano spent several years on active duty as a naval reserve officer. He carries the permanent rank of Commander, U.S. Navy—Retired. Returning to civilian life, he joined Alexander Grant & Company (now Grant Thornton), a large public accounting firm. Following nearly 8 years as a practicing CPA, he entered the corporate world, eventually holding senior financial management positions with Computer Sciences Corporation, Epson America, and several smaller companies. In 1986, he founded Western Management Associates, the consulting business that he owns and operates today. In his practice, he often serves as the part-time chief financial officer for client companies, and from that grew the trademark of his business, "Your CFO for Rent."

When not in the office, Mr. Siciliano has served a number of non-profit organizations—both professional and charitable—as chairman of the board, board member, and treasurer, and he is most often drawn to organizations that help children. In addition to occasional gourmet cooking, he enjoys tennis and the theater in his spare time, both available in abundance near his home in Redondo Beach, California. He can be reached at 310-645-1091 or gene@CFOforRent.com or by visiting his websites at www.CFOforRent.com or www.Gene Siciliano.com.

1

Why This Book Was Written and Why You Should Read It

You are in a magnificent profession—the teaching of our children. The role of the teacher, in my opinion, is one of the most valuable in our society. For those of us who are raising children, a caring teacher is far more important than the quarterback on Sunday's televised football game. Yet the average salary of a professional football player in 2009 is estimated to be 17 times the average teacher's salary.[1] A survey by the American Federation of Teachers in 2005 found virtually the same numbers, indicating essentially no growth in the intervening years. As this is written, teachers are being furloughed and new hiring frozen all over the country as part of some school districts' efforts to compensate for drastically reduced funding. We value our teachers so much that teaching is consistently in the top 10 most respected professions. Yet we consistently turn down bond measures for educational improvements across the country. Many school systems throughout the nation are so anxious to attract teachers that some will even pay off student loans to get them. Yet

---

1. Median salary of K–12 teachers is under $45,000 nationally, according to http://www.payscale.com/research/US/All_K-12_Teachers/Salary. Median salary of professional football players is $770,000, according to http://wiki.answers.com/Q/What_is_the_average_salary_of_an_NFL_football_player.

elsewhere teachers are losing their jobs because of money shortages in their districts.

We can't change that overnight, unfortunately. My hope is we can change it during your career so you can see the fruits of that greater respect translating into greater compensation for every good, dedicated, committed teacher. However, while we're hoping, and hopefully writing to newspaper editors, state and federal legislators, and school board presidents, you need to create a life for yourself and your family and to make it work financially with what you have and what you're earning today.

For most Americans, finance is a foreign language. For nonfinancial professionals, their education in finance might have been a college course or two, most of it having nothing to do with the personal financial affairs that figure so prominently in our lives. Teachers and college instructors at all levels are not much different in that regard from the rest of the country. Yet your personal finances are one of the most important matters you must deal with in your life, and your decisions will help determine whether your life will be well provided for or a constant struggle to make ends meet. This is not a good set of options for someone in such an important career. Perhaps if this were a more socialist society, the government would have made all teachers wards of the state, and you'd have nothing to worry about (or to hope for, not incidentally). Since America is a free society with a capitalist economy, you are left to make your own mistakes and learn as you go along. Corwin and I both think that you deserve better, and that's why this book was written.

If there's one thing that education has taught us, it's that we don't have to learn everything the hard way. My dad taught me how to ride a bike so I wouldn't fall so often learning by myself. Learning to count when I started school made it much easier to do math when that became important soon thereafter. I believe the tools and explanations in this book will help you in a very significant way to get a head start on mastering your finances and building your own personal wealth. That doesn't mean I'm promising you a retirement villa in Italy and a summer place in the Hamptons, but it does mean this: If you use the lessons in this book, you will be well on your way to maximizing your opportunities to live a comfortable life and a secure retirement. That, to me, is financial mastery.

My business is helping nonfinancial people learn the power of financial tools to improve their lives and businesses. I work with CEOs of companies and the managers within those companies. I speak to small business owners all across the country, who rely on their businesses to support their families and the families of their employees. The focus is always to help clients and audiences learn the tools, help them learn how and when to use them, and guide them in making it work for them every day. Then I write to make the same tools available to people who can't hire my company's financial experts or participate in one of my workshops.

For the remainder of this book, consider that you are in a personal workshop dedicated to honoring your profession and helping you to be appropriately compensated for all your hard work and dedication to our children. Thank you.

2

Your Personal Business Plan

The Master Road Map

Setting Goals

You've probably heard it a hundred times or more. Depending on the grade you teach, you might even have told your students how important it is to set goals for themselves—being on time to class, making the team, achieving high school graduation, earning a university diploma, making career choices, or even landing a first job. We all talk about, and generally appreciate, the value of setting goals for our businesses and our careers, maybe even saving for the down payment on our next home. But how about financial goals as a pattern for your personal life and career? Considering the average salary of a teacher today, even though it has crept up in recent years, you need to make some serious choices if you want to live a full life and then enjoy a comfortable retirement. Choices made in our heads that don't get out of our heads frequently get lost in our heads, victims of the next thing on our endless to-do lists.

Goals work when we make them clear and visible and when we work them with discipline. In fact, there is an acronym I like that conveys the characteristics of goals that work for us. Developed for business owners and CEOs, it's just as relevant for you and your family. The acronym is *SMART* and it looks like this:

S = Specific targets—for example, an amount of money in the bank, an investment portfolio of X, twice as much as I had on Y date, and so forth. Choosing a goal that simply says you want to "make more money" doesn't count.

M = Measurable—something you can actually track so you can keep a record of your progress. Money in the bank works; annual income earned works; "getting better" at your job doesn't work.

A = Achievable—a goal that is reasonably within reach, albeit a stretch, so your mind doesn't tell itself the goal is nonsense. If that happens, the mind shuts down, and perception becomes reality.

R = Relevant—relates to where you want to go financially. If your end objective is to have a retirement fund in place, setting a goal to take a European vacation each year might not contribute, while a goal to take up skiing might be fun but irrelevant to your financial goals. This is not to say you can't have those things, but they are incidental to meeting your goals, and that may say something about their priority in the grand scheme of things.

T = Time sensitive—Here's the date that goal will be met; the month or the day or the year doesn't matter as long as it's exact and it meets the other criteria.

While goals go by a lot of names—objectives, targets, goals, priorities, commitments—they are in their simplest form either things we hope to accomplish soon or those we hope to accomplish later on. So we'll try not to get hung up on terminology here. If you really want it, it's a goal.

Short Term Versus Long Term

I think of short term as being anything to be accomplished in the next 12 months, and a long-term goal is anything that I expect will take longer than a year. That helps us to organize our thinking.

Next concept: Short-term goals should be steps along the way to achieving long-term goals. For example, a short-term goal might be putting $500 a month into a savings account designed to become that first-home down payment. If the needed down payment is $20,000, then the long-term goal might be to buy that home in 3½ years, since $500 a month will become $20,000 in 3 years and 4 months.

As a general rule, I suggest that your short-term goals should directly support your long-term goals, as in my example, so that your day-to-day commitment is to the short-term goals. If you do that, the long-term goals will pretty much take care of themselves.

Keep this in mind: *You can't achieve a long-term goal;* you can only take small steps today in the direction of a long-term goal. Achieve all the small steps, and the long-term goal is handled. Five hundred dollars a month for 40 months is the down payment. Goal achievement is about the $500 for this month.

So how do we go about developing the ultimate financial goal-setting tool, a budget? Very early in my working life, before there was a computer or two in virtually every home, my wife and I developed a budget to help us save money for the down payment on our first home. We did it on paper, columnar paper on which I handwrote all the entries for the budget *and* all the amounts we actually spent money on. Each expenditure was counted—check by check—to produce the reports we used to see how we were doing on our plan. There was no bookkeeping software and no electronic spreadsheet to help, only a sharp pencil and a very big eraser. We were really dedicated in those days. While your budget doesn't have to be that labor intensive today, a budget still involves some work. By the way, we saved the money, and we got the house. Technology would have just made it easier.

How to Do It

I'm going to assume you buy the premise that a budget is the best tool for planning and achieving a financial goal, or you would have stopped reading by now. So the next big question is, how? Let's lay out a process for developing your financial plan.

1. Decide what your goal is and when you want to be there. Don't think about how you're going to get there for now, just put the goal down on paper so you can see it and feel comfortable that it's SMARTly stated. *Example:* You want to be living in your own home in 5 years, and the home will be a three-bedroom, two-bath home within 10 miles of your work and 2 miles of an elementary school.

2. Validate the data you need to clarify your goal from a financial perspective. Contact a real estate agent and ask him or her what you should expect to pay for such a home today. Never mind that the market will be different in 5 years. It will always be different, and today is all you have to work with, so use it. Your broker-to-be tells you the typical price for that type of home runs between $200,000 and $350,000, depending on the neighborhood, the age of the house, and whatever. You decide to shoot for $300,000 as the price you'll be prepared to pay.

3. Your broker-to-be also tells you to plan for a 20% down payment and closing costs of $3,000. That's $63,000 you'll need to have in the bank. Over 48 months, you'll need to save on average $1,312 a month. Yikes! That's never going to happen, you decide. You need to adjust the goal. This is a normal element of planning—the goal has to appear reasonably attainable for everyone involved to believe in it. Otherwise, you will not get there. "Stuff" will get in the way, other things will take a higher priority in the moment, and so on. We all find ways to sabotage goals we don't really believe in.

4. So you revise the plan. The time line is now 6 years, and you'll start out in the $275,000 range. Now the front-end money is only $58,000 over 72 months, and that works out to $806 a month. You decide you can do that. Your first goal has been established and reduced to a short-term goal that will lead to the long-term goal. Now you can get to work on your next goal.

Matching the Goals and the Money

Just as we did in the example, you will define each key goal you have, with details and a time line and an estimated amount. It doesn't matter if they're estimates that are likely to change. You work with what you have, and you adjust your course along the way. The key is to have a course and to keep on it until there is reason to change. Your family financial plan should outline each key goal that is meaningful for you and put them all down on paper. Your own mind—your logic, your feelings, your emotions—will tell you if the goal, the amount, and the time line are reasonable and attainable, really relevant to the life you want to create for yourself, and worth working for.

A key element of your plan, as you can see from the example, is that you have to put a dollar amount on the goal so you know what you're working toward in exact terms. How much money do you need to save this month? How much money do you need to invest this year? Is it worth shortening or even giving up the vacation trip you planned for this summer in order to meet this year's target in your plan? You may decide that it isn't, but at least you'll be making that decision consciously instead of accidentally. And that is a keystone of successful planning. It's not about drafting a plan that will never change. It's about drafting a plan that will change when we choose to change it and for reasons that we consider appropriate in the circumstances.

OK, now that your financial goals have been defined and you have a plan to get there (sort of), how do you make this into a month-to-month management tool to actually reach the goal? How do you build a budget? Here's how to set up a budget and how to make it work for you.

Creating Your Family Budget

The next step is converting your list of goals into a budget. The budget is the working tool that you'll use to track your progress each month, and it is built around the simple idea that you define what you earn, and then you decide what you will spend that income on, line by line, month by month, including the amounts you will save or invest to reach the financial goals you've set for yourself. So let's make a list of all the income and expense items that will form the basis for our budget.

A fairly obvious assumption is that you can only spend what you earn. That really means what you bring home after income taxes and state employment-related taxes, because you don't have much leeway with taxes. So *income* is the first thing on our list. Depending on the practice in your school district, you will get one or two paychecks a month, maybe three a few times a year. That's the first item in your budget, just like the income statement of a big company. If you do some tutoring or have some savings income today, list those as well.

🔑 KEY POINT

If you work in a state where you don't get a paycheck over the summer months and you don't get work elsewhere, your challenge may be to save enough in the other nine months to make up for the dry summer when it may be impossible to save.

Next are *uncontrollable expenses,* the things you must spend money for and for which the amount is more or less fixed, like the following:

- The apartment rent or mortgage payment
- Life insurance
- The electric and gas bills and any other mostly uncontrollable utilities

Next we'll list all the things that your financial plan says you want to have money for—your goals. List them individually because we'll treat them individually in our budget. We put these ahead of the remaining expenses that you have every month for a reason. A critical concept: *You pay yourself first, not last.* If the goal is important, and if the timetable is important, then it must be considered something akin to an uncontrollable expense. You do it first before you go shopping or to the movies or on vacation. And for those who would argue that shopping for food is not an option, I will ask you if you've ever had the experience that you could spend more or less for food depending on how much money you had to spend. If the answer is yes, then you know what I mean.

So now enter the items that are not so set in stone, about which you have some discretion or a lot of discretion. Yes, that includes food. We'll call these *controllable expenses* because they can vary and often do based on how much income we have to spend at the time. Groceries, clothes for the family, health insurance premiums (because you can adjust your benefits as your needs change), cable/satellite TV, household repairs, entertainment, and so on might all fall into this category.

All right, you have your list. Let's put it into a format that we can work with. If you have some familiarity with Microsoft Excel or any similar spreadsheet program, that's the best tool to use. Better yet, use the online Excel model created for you at www.corwin.com/financial mastery. Whichever method you decide to use, it's time to type your list into the spreadsheet. The list goes down the left column of your spreadsheet because you'll have time periods across the top in a matrix look, which spreadsheets are ideally suited for. See Table 2.1 for an example of what your spreadsheet might look like when it's completely laid out.

Even though you're making long-term plans with your finances, the budget example shows only a few months of activity. I recommend you set it up only for 1 year at a time, 12 months across the top, for two reasons:

1. It's difficult to work with a spreadsheet with too many columns across (especially your first one).

2. Your budget will be different next year just because life does that. You'll likely want to allocate your income somewhat differently, and it's simpler to set up a new spreadsheet than to try to adjust the old one to the new spending pattern.

"This is hard." One thing is true for obvious reasons: Something we've never done before is usually hard to do the first time. When you first consider a budget as a money management tool, especially if numbers aren't particularly your strong area, it may seem really hard, incredibly detailed, maybe even a little anal. No one you know does this. Why should you? You don't know what you spent on groceries last month, so how can you budget for it this month? You've never written details into your checkbook when you buy something; you just write the check. Now you need to remember what it was for so you can decide

Table 2.1 The Family Budget

	January	February	March	April	May	June
Income						
Paycheck after taxes	6,650	6,650	6,650	6,650	8,275	5,650
Private tutoring fees	300	300	300	300	300	—
Interest from savings account	25	26	27	28	29	30
Subtotal income	6,975	6,976	6,977	6,978	8,604	5,680
Uncontrollable expenses						
Rent	1,800	1,800	1,800	1,800	1,800	1,800
Electricity and gas	200	200	175	175	175	175
Child care	1,000	1,000	1,000	1,000	1,000	1,000
Life insurance premiums	400	400	400	400	400	400
Subtotal uncontrollable	3,400	3,400	3,375	3,375	3,375	3,375
Goals						
House down payment fund	900	900	900	900	900	900
401(k) contribution	350	350	350	350	350	350
Investment fund	500	500	500	500	500	500
Subtotal goals	1,750	1,750	1,750	1,750	1,750	1,750
Controllable expenses						
Groceries	350	350	350	350	350	350
Clothes	—	—	—	—	250	—
Medical expenses	200	200	200	200	200	200
Health insurance premiums	550	550	550	550	550	550
TV subscription	75	75	75	75	75	75
Dinners out and entertainment	200	200	200	200	200	200
Gifts for birthdays and holidays	—	—	200	—	—	200
Health club membership	75	75	75	75	75	75
School-related expenses	50	50	50	50	50	—
Vacation trip	—	—	—	—	—	500
Subtotal controllable	1,500	1,500	1,700	1,500	1,750	2,150
Cash left over, or short	325	326	152	353	1,729	(1,595)
Cumulative total during the year	325	651	803	1,156	2,885	1,290

if you want it in your budget or not. You will be tempted to toss the whole thing out the window. This is crazy! There has to be a better way!

No, actually, there's not. There are different ways to manage your money, but the ones that work best are all variations of a budget, incorporating the discipline to decide ahead of time what to spend money on and what not to and when. The good news is that it's not the end of the known world if you miss the budgeted target and over-spend a few items in a month, because a budget enables you to make up for it next month or adjust the spending target for something else in your budget or adjust the timing of the goal a bit if necessary. It's a plan, not a monument. It doesn't have to be cast in concrete. But if you miss the target consistently, you can pretty much assume the ulti-mate goal is moving out on your time line, maybe beyond reach.

Once you have entered your list into the spreadsheet, and the monthly columns have been labeled as in the example, start entering numbers onto each line in the column that represents the month in which money will be spent. Rent money will go into every monthly column, while back-to-school clothes will likely be spent only in late summer. How much to enter? Start with what you spent last time, referring to your checkbook or past credit card statements. Later you'll have the opportunity to adjust your starting numbers to current reality.

Next, add up each column's income and expenditures and record the totals on the respective subtotal lines so you can see how much each section makes up of the whole.

Finally, add the income subtotals and subtract the expense and investment subtotals to tell you how the whole year should work out. Adding the monthly *cash left over* for all preceding months together on the last line as you proceed through the year will give you the cumulative totals as well, and your model is done. Sit back and look at what you've done.

Your objective is to try to make each month come out at zero or better, but they won't always—the vacation month, remember, or the holidays—so the next best thing is to make sure the cumulative totals come out zero or better or have some extra cash at the beginning of the year that will tide you over any negative months so you finish the year where you want to be.

OK, now a small realization will come to you the first time you do this. It won't come out right at the bottom. You'll have more money left over in some months than you think is possible, or you have spent more than you make, not a good plan for financial security. So you'll need to go back and adjust the numbers, plan to spend less here, more there, and less way over there until you get the right totals at the bottom. This doesn't mean you drop in numbers that you know are silly and unattainable. You make changes that you can manage, usually in the section called *controllable expenses* (note the sheer logic of that label). When you're done adjusting your plan details, you will have a picture of your spending plan for the next 12 months.

This is now your budget, and the idea is to have something left over after all the expenses and your goals are covered to give you the opportunity to be truly frivolous without feeling guilty. Of course if the bottom comes out to zero, that's still a big win. You've provided for your long-term goals, paid the bills, and gotten another year closer to financial security. Hip, hip, hooray!

Watching It Work: Sticking to It

Let's take a look at a hypothetical budget for Ms. Sanchez, a career teacher with a family, who was an early buyer of this book. At the end of the first month living with her new budget, she'll have her first opportunity to see how well she's controlling her money. By a strange coincidence, Ms. Sanchez's budget is identical with Table 2.1. While she would plan her budget for the entire 12 months of the year, we've shown only 6 months here just to get it to fit on the page.

As you can see, Ms. Sanchez planned her expenses as she thinks she'll spend the money. She budgeted vacation money in the summer and gifts when the occasions come up on her calendar. This is a better approach than simply dividing each annual expense by 12 to arrive at an average monthly expense because she can really measure each month as it is expected to happen.

It's time to compare what she earned and spent with what she planned. She can do this in her head if she's better with numbers than I am, or she can do it on paper so she can study the result and decide what to do about it, if anything. Table 2.2 is the format I suggest for that analysis, and if you've visited the website that accompanies the book, www.corwin.com/financialmastery, you'll see that the Family Budget model has a year's worth of pages to enable you to create this comparison with relative ease. It follows the format of Ms. Sanchez's budget, and it allows her to see the impact of each line item on the bottom-line result.

The first column of numbers, labeled *Actual,* is what actually happened during the month—our teacher's actual take-home pay before insurance deductions, her actual expenses, and actual contributions to her goals accounts. The second column of numbers is the budget for that month, just as she developed it earlier. The third column is the difference between the *Actual* and *Budget,* representing the amount by which she overspent or underspent that month.

And that third column is the most important one. It's where she should do the studying. In my example, income and controllable

Table 2.2	Budget Variance Analysis		
January 2010	**Actual**	**Budget**	**Difference**
Income			
Paycheck after taxes	6,650	6,650	—
Private tutoring fees	250	300	50
Interest from savings account	24	25	1
Subtotal income	6,924	6,975	51
Uncontrollable expenses			
Rent	1,800	1,800	—
Electricity and gas	185	200	15
Child care	1,000	1,000	—
Life insurance premiums	396	400	4
Subtotal uncontrollable	3,381	3,400	19
Goals			
House down payment fund	900	900	—
401(k) contribution	350	350	—
Investment fund	500	500	—
Subtotal goals	1,750	1,750	—
Controllable expenses			
Groceries	396	350	(46)
Clothes	200	—	(200)
Medical expenses	—	200	200
Health insurance premiums	548	550	2
TV subscription	75	75	—
Dinners out and entertainment	225	200	(25)
Gifts for birthdays and holidays	—	—	—
Health club membership	75	75	—
School-related expenses	55	50	(5)
Vacation trip	—	—	—
Subtotal controllable	1,574	1,500	(74)
Cash left over, or short	**219**	**325**	**106**
Cumulative total during the year	219	325	106

expenses came in nominally different from plan—a good result. Controllable expenses, by contrast, were saved only because the kids had no medical bills that month, thankfully. She might want to keep a closer eye on things like clothes shopping and entertainment until she gets some of that frivolous money in the bank.

If Ms. Sanchez goes through this little study exercise each month and modifies her spending patterns based on what she learns, it will get easier and easier to keep within budget *and* to create the next year's budget. And her goals will be in the bag or the bank.

One final thought about process here: Once each year, you and Ms. Sanchez should revisit your long-range plan to see that it still makes sense to you. That is the opportunity to make any changes indicated in your plan and to prepare your next monthly budget based on that review. Such changes could include a salary increase, a rent increase, a shift from one health plan to another, and so on. So when you change your smoke alarm batteries, review your budget too.

Adjusting for Change
Because There Always Is Some

Now that you have a plan and a budget, all you have to do is follow it to the goal, right? That's true in theory but easier said than done for a whole host of reasons, among them these:

- Investment risk, evidenced by the stock market and real estate volatility of the past few years, may cause you to adjust the timing or the amounts that will ultimately be available.
- Your spending and saving discipline: How many times can you cut corners on what you spend or what you save before you begin impacting the end goal?
- Unexpected emergencies truly require a readjustment of thinking because they demand an instant—often financial—response.
- You will make intentional changes in your plan because the situation has changed—the house down payment is in the bank; you need to adjust the plan for a (larger) monthly mortgage payment now.

This is a bit like *The Little Engine That Could.* (Do you still use that story?) Each time you look at your progress and wonder if you'll ever get there, or you've had an unexpected expense or change in your income, you have an opportunity to either throw the plan out or sit down and look at it with today's eyes. Ask yourself these three questions:

1. Have your goals changed?

2. Do you still want them as badly as when you first wrote them down?

3. If you were making a brand-new plan *today*, what would you do differently to get there?

Once you have answered those questions, you have just revised your plan to take into account all that has happened up until now. Write it down and begin following the new, revised plan, because without a plan, your chances of reaching your goals are truly up to chance. If you've been to Las Vegas, you know how that works out.

It's time to decide. This is where you separate yourself from all the folks who will years from now be lamenting how the system kept them from getting ahead, how they tried but just couldn't make the compromises and, yes, sacrifices that seemed to be needed to save enough for a good retirement. When you meet one of these people in the supermarket or at a social gathering, what will your story be? Will you be comfortably retired, with your children educated and on their way, or will you be sharing sad stories with the others who didn't quite make it. You get to write that story today. And tomorrow. And the next day. In fact, you get to decide one day at a time how your life will turn out, starting today.

Which path will you choose?

SUMMARY OF KEY IDEAS FOR CHAPTER 2

1. The SMART goals acronym helps us to define meaningful goals that we can actually achieve.

2. A household budget helps us to make carefully thought-out decisions about how we'll spend our income so we can avoid the more emotionally driven spending decisions we often make spontaneously. It also gives us a tool for keeping track of how we're doing on sticking with our budget.

3. When developing your budget, it's important to separately group uncontrollable expenses, goals, and controllable expenses, because you will assign different priorities to each group, depending on the income you have available. Uncontrollable expenses must be paid, goals must get priority if they're important to you, and controllable expenses come last.

4. A budget variance report compares what your budget said you'd earn and spend with what actually happened so you can see and find a way to manage the differences. A few items overspent are easily corrected; a pattern of overspending says you're not living within your budget, and your goals are likely to suffer as a result.

5. As time goes by, you are likely to find the need to change your budget to keep in line with reality. Adjust for needed changes and move on—that's a normal part of life. Deciding the system just won't let you succeed is self-defeating.

3

Managing Your Paycheck

The Source

For most people in the teaching profession, your main source of income is the paycheck from your school district. Some of you have been able to add other options such as tutoring, writing, and even multilevel marketing. Most of those other options probably produce less income than your salary and are more erratic. As a result, for nearly all teachers, the bulk of your financial planning will center on the salary you get paid as a teacher. All the guidance in this chapter is aimed squarely at managing that salary, but at the same time these thoughts can be applied to ancillary income as well.

Setting Up Your Payroll Deductions

Income Taxes

Filling out a federal Form W-4 to tell the payroll department how to handle your paycheck is pretty simple. The more exemptions you claim, the less will be withheld from your paycheck for income taxes. The thinking behind what you put on the form is worth a few words to explain some of the options that are available to you.

First of all, the exemptions you are asked to claim are not intended to be calculated based on the number of people in your family. You may have a family of three and legitimately claim eight exemptions on your W-4. The intent of the exemption declaration is to achieve pay-as-you-go income tax collection. The effect is to give you an opportunity to choose whether you want your tax bill at the end of the year to come out even—no tax due and no refund—or if you want to get a refund or write a check. It's all up to you—and all legal to a point. You can find out exactly how much will be deducted from your paycheck for 1, 3, or 12 exemptions by downloading *Publication 15, Circular E, Employer's Tax Guide* (available at www.irs.gov).

If you claim zero exemptions, for example, you are probably assured of getting a refund when you file your tax return. Of course that means you are getting back your own money that you loaned to the government interest free for a year, but for some people, it's a way to force some savings.

If instead you claim 12 exemptions, or whatever number will reduce your income tax withholding to a very tiny number, you'll take home more money each month, and you will be on the hook for the difference when you file your return. You may also be subject to a $500 penalty for overstating the exemptions that you are entitled to. It's best to aim for something that gets you close to breakeven when you file your tax return at year-end. To do that, use the tables in the IRS booklet above to find the withholding amount that will, when you multiply it times the number of paychecks you will get during the year, add up to the total amount of income tax you expect to pay based on your income. Last year's tax return may be a good starting point for that number.

Once you get past the taxes (other than income tax, the other tax deductions are automatic), there are several other options to have money taken out of your check for various things—health insurance, 401(k) plans, credit union contributions, and more. We'll discuss most of these as they become relevant to the chapter topic.

Health Plan Deductions

In an effort to help companies keep their health care costs under control and still provide for their employees' needs, Congress has authorized a series of programs in which employees are able to allocate money for a variety of medical and other health care costs out of money that is not taxed by the IRS. They carry labels such as FSA (flexible spending account), HRA (health reimbursement arrangement), and HSA (health savings account), all of which are shorthand for their much longer names. Contributions to these plans are not counted when calculating payroll taxes. This allows a company or a school district to offer valuable benefits at a lower cost to the employee (who doesn't have to pay for it out of what's left after income tax withholding) and to the employer (who doesn't have to pay employer payroll taxes either).

How they work: The employer offers a plan, which is administered by a third-party company, and the employee decides how much of the covered health care expenses he or she wants to provide for through payroll deduction. The amounts deducted can be used for expenses not covered by the district's normal health care plans, such as chiropractic, vision, or dental care, and even dependent care expenses. The employer in effect keeps the amounts contributed for the employee and reimburses the employee for covered expenses as they arise. If the amounts deducted from paychecks aren't used up in the year, some of these plans will allow the balance to be carried over to the next year.

There are lots of options to these plans, far too many to go into detail here. But you'll find some excellent descriptive information at websites of plan administrators, such as www.secureoneinc.com. If you anticipate incurring expenses that your health plan won't cover—perhaps because you or your school district has chosen a high-deductible health plan—it's worth your time to research these options before you decide what to do.

Retirement Plan Deductions

There is a perception for most of us that makes this chapter seem particularly challenging—our paychecks never seem big enough for all the things we want to do with them. That's what makes America's workforce such a poor saving group compared to just about every other nation on the planet. Sometimes it seems that the check has been spent or spoken for as soon as it comes out of the envelope, and we grimace if we learn that another $10 is being deducted for some wrinkle in the tax rules or an increase in our health insurance premium. (Uh, that would be more than $10. Wouldn't it?) And yet there are some real opportunities to build savings by taking a few dollars a month and socking them away before we get to spend them. A good application of the *out of sight, out of mind* rule is to have it put aside for you before you even see it.

One of the keystone concepts on which this book is based is the idea that a small amount of money regularly put aside can make the difference between a comfortable retirement and a parsimonious one. Chapter 7 will demonstrate this principle dramatically with the law of compound interest. But it starts here, with your paycheck, today. As hard as it must seem to think about retirement planning if your career has barely gotten started, this is exactly the time to think about it. Investment planning and retirement planning are just that—planning. Every plan requires resources to give it life, and the resources you put aside today, at the early stages of your career, will be the least costly and the most beneficial of your life. Let's cover some of those opportunities now.

401(k) Plans

These plans are part of a long-term government initiative to increase the rate of savings among American workers and shelter them from dependence on company retirement plans that may not be there when they need them. They can also be one of the best savings bargains you'll ever find if your employer provides matching contributions. What does that mean? A school district (or city or state) with a 401(k) plan is providing you an option to save money in a systematic way directly from your paycheck. In some cases, this may also be the closest thing to a pension plan that the school district can afford, and many organizations have scrapped their pension plans in the past decade in favor of these plans. They're simpler for employers to administer and less costly to fund.

Here's the sweetener, the gift, the icing on the cake. Many employers, with the encouragement of Uncle Sam, provide additional money to match part of what you contribute to the plan, money that ultimately become yours without having to pay income tax on it as long as it stays in the account. Some employers will contribute up to 50 cents for every dollar you contribute, and after some period of continuous employment, that money is yours to take with you when you leave that job. *Thanks, Uncle!* This is a great way to get a head start on above-average investment returns—you're automatically up 20%, 25%, or 50% as long as you're in the plan and on the job. And the combined amount earns for you as well, assuming your company has invested those funds in income-producing assets.

Aha! There is a pothole here to watch for! What does the school district invest those funds in during the period you are contributing and working away busily in your classroom? Options typically include money market funds, mutual funds, and perhaps individual stocks as well. They get to choose what options you will have, but they have to honor the choices you make from among those options. Yet some companies will restrict the options they offer unreasonably, potentially making your choices less viable. A few years ago, Enron Corporation had most of its employees' money invested in the stock of the company itself. When Enron went under, so did the 401(k)s of many of its employees.

So big caveat here: Study carefully the investment choices you are asked to make when you enroll in your district's 401(k) plan. Don't just pick the money market fund, and don't narrow your choices too much so that the reversal of fortunes of a single company could endanger your investment. Chapter 10 will discuss investment choices in some detail, and that will help you here as well.

OK, second caveat: If your school district offers 401(k) debit cards to encourage employees to join the plan, *do not take one.* Debit cards are sometimes offered to enable employees to more easily exercise their legal right to borrow against their 401(k)s. That's the good news and the bad news. Ease of borrowing against your retirement fund is never a good idea unless it's absolutely the source of last resort. It's too easy to not pay it back and thus deplete a key retirement resource. Better to find another way, or make borrowing against this fund a hassle, so you'll think twice before doing it.

My Recommendation: If your employer matches at all, contribute as much as you can to get their full match. It's found money that will at some point be entirely yours even if you leave that school district.

IRAs: The Essential First Step in Retirement Planning

The first major effort the federal government made to induce Americans to save for their own retirement (probably designed when they first discovered that Social Security was going to be in trouble down the road) was the IRA (individual retirement account). Originally offered in only one flavor, its popularity gave rise to a new version later on, not better but definitely different. And many of us will have occasion to use both over our working lives.

Traditional IRA: Deductible Contributions, Taxable Withdrawals. This is the original. You open a qualified savings account at a bank or securities firm and make deposits of up to $2,000 a year into that account, and the federal government will allow you to claim a $2,000 deduction on your income taxes, the maximum contribution in 2009. Think about that for a minute. This is like giving money to charity and getting to deduct it on your taxes, except that you are the charity. And even better, as that money earns interest, dividends, or whatever income it produces in the years ahead, you don't have to pay taxes on that money until you withdraw it in your retirement years, when your tax rate will likely be much lower. That's called tax-deferred income, a very good thing for us taxpayers.

While not quite as enticing as a 401(k) contribution that your employer matches, it's the next best thing. And when you get older, the amount you can contribute and deduct goes up. In 2009, folks over 50 could sock away $6,000 and deduct it all. Those over 49 could put away $5,000. There are a couple of caveats: Being enrolled in a company retirement plan could limit or eliminate your ability to have an IRA. If you and your spouse make too much money, you can't take the deduction. If you withdraw money before you reach age 59½, there is a 10% early withdrawal penalty. And you have to start taking it out, and paying taxes on it, when you turn 70½.

My Recommendation: In my opinion, if you are a working person intending to live long enough to retire, you should contribute to some type of IRA every year.

Roth IRA: Taxable Contributions, Tax-Free Withdrawals. This is the new flavor that was introduced in 1997 to give workers with a company retirement plan an opportunity to supplement their retirement savings in a tax-deferred way. You don't get a deduction when you make your contribution, but you don't pay tax on later withdrawals either. Here's the best part, though: You don't pay taxes on the earnings in your Roth IRA account either, not now or when you withdraw them later. None, zip, zero. *Tax free* is even better than *tax deferred*, if you get my meaning. As for the bookkeeping, it's pretty simple to manage when every dollar you withdraw is tax free—you just take it out and spend it. That's all. And one more thing: If your school district has a great retirement plan, good for you. You can *still* have a Roth IRA!

My Recommendation: If you can get along without the tax deduction for your annual contributions *and* you expect your income at age 70 to still be pretty high, opt for the Roth IRA instead of the traditional IRA. The numbers will usually work out better.

There are a couple other IRA flavors, which I'm not going to try to squeeze into this book, called nondeductible, traditional IRAs (a lot like the Roth IRA) and SEP-IRAs (a simplified employee pension individual retirement account for self-employed folks). Ask your tax preparer to explain these to you if you don't qualify for one of the others or the breadwinner is self-employed. As for what to invest your IRA money in, check out Chapters 7, 9, and 10 for the most common ways to put your IRA money to work.

Rollovers: An Opportunity and a Caveat. When you leave one employer where you have contributed to a retirement plan, you get to take the retirement plan contributions with you, including your own contributions and whatever of the employer's contributions have *vested* in your name (become yours permanently). How you do that can have significant tax consequences. *Rollover* is the term used to describe what happens when money you have invested in a 401(k) or IRA is moved from one tax-advantaged plan to another, such as a different IRA or your new school district's 401(k) plan. Rollover also refers to moving

IRA funds from one IRA account to another, where no employer is involved, but it's still one tax-advantaged plan to another. If you do it right, you will have no tax consequences. If you do it wrong, the IRS will wag its finger at you and take a big bite out of your funds. The key is making sure the money goes into the receiving account directly and within the time frame spelled out in IRS rules, usually 60 days. Since 401(k)s are easier to borrow from, but IRAs give you more control of the investment choices, you should talk over any transfer choices with your tax adviser before making the move.

Spending Less Than You Earn: Ideas for Stretching Your Dollars!

It won't be surprising to learn that expenses, left unmonitored, tend to grow. Think about your cell phone bill today compared to a year or two ago. And how about your cable or satellite TV bill—same as it was? It could be, since the average cost of both those services has actually dropped over the past couple years. But interestingly, the average size of the monthly bill an American family pays has increased because of all the add-ons.[1] This is particularly insidious for expenses that we pay for automatically through a credit card charge or direct bank withdrawal. The convenience of that automatic payment is the enemy of expense control, especially when money is tight. You can probably think of examples in your household budget that you could do without—or already are—but that you are still paying for every month.

And then there's the family car, or vehicle, I should say, based on the number of trucks and SUVs still in family driveways. Given the price of gas these days, I'm surprised more of these aren't sitting on used-car lots. But more important, a great way to save money is to drive your family car another couple years before trading it in on a new one. I'm not a big fan of changing cars every 3 years—I'm driving a wonderfully reliable car I bought over 9 years ago, which may seem a bit extreme. But it runs beautifully, and any minor repairs or upkeep are much less than a monthly car payment. I live near a large aerospace company in Los Angeles, and I'm amazed how many of their well-paid (I assume) workers come to work every morning in 10- to 15-year-old cars that look a little worn around the edges but are probably saving their engineer drivers a ton of money. Ford Motor's chief economist reported in a recent webinar that the average age for cars on the road is 9.4 years. Shucks, I'm not so extreme after all. How about you?

---

1. *Wall Street Journal*, January 28, 2009, Family Money column, p. D8.

Here's another idea worth thinking about. Going grocery shopping? Go online and type *supermarket coupons* into your browser. I found a list of 760,000 websites that offer coupons on products you may buy every week, many of them coupons that you can either print or download to your supermarket rewards card to save you money when you get to the store. I read of one woman who saved $50 on a $120 shopping bill with just such coupons that she said took her 15 to 20 minutes to find. Let's see, 15 minutes and a $50 return; that's $200 an hour. All right, maybe it doesn't quite work that way, and maybe it feels a bit old-fashioned, but you get the point. You can save money in so many places if you just look for the opportunities, especially in today's economy where retailers are working overtime to get consumers spending again.

And then there's bargain shopping. Most of us think of bargain shopping as wandering around the stores looking for sales or scanning the newspaper and latest load of junk mail when we are ready to buy something that we need. If you're Internet savvy, you also do that shopping online at Amazon.com or a host of virtual referral sites like overstock.com or bizrate.com. A *USA Today* article[2] suggests a more organized and effective approach: Buy things when the dealers are most anxious to sell them, not when you most need to have them. The most familiar example of this is buying a new car—shopping for this year's model in December just as next year's models are coming out and the dealer is trying to make room for them. But this same approach can work with lots of other purchases as well, if you plan your purchases as much as a year in advance and buy them when the dealers most want to sell. According to industry experts, here are the best times to buy some big-ticket items using that same philosophy:

The Purchase	Best Time(s)	Why?
Furniture	January and July	New shipments are about to arrive at dealers' showrooms.
Jewelry and diamonds	July	Summer is traditionally very slow for jewelry sales; July is the nadir.
Patio furniture and plants	August	Summer selling is over, and dealers want to clear the floor.
New car purchase—current model	December mid-month	It's the slowest period of the year for dealers.
Baby products	February through April	Dealers offer the most sales during these months.

---

2. *USA Today*, September 4, 2009, "Plan purchases a year out to get bargains," Managing Your Money, p. 3B.

Getting Your Kids on Board With Your Finances

One of the age-old debates is about whether you should shelter your kids from the real family financial situation—and somehow find a way to take care of their needs without them knowing how hard it is—or share the reality with them. I suggest the best approach is the sharing option. Your kids can sense when something is wrong even if you don't mention it, and chances are their friends' families are experiencing some of the same challenges you are, even if they're not teachers. Here's how to get your kids to be part of the solution and prepare them for their own financial futures:

- Stop using credit cards and pay cash for most everything, particularly when the kids are around. Plastic doesn't seem as real as cash to kids, and cash is practical and reassuring. Consider layaway plans too.
- Encourage part-time employment as a way for them to get extra money. It's the fastest way for them to understand the exchange of resources that employment represents, and it presents an opportunity for them to start a savings program or pay for some household expenses they can relate to.
- When you decide you can't afford something they're used to having, explain to them in financial terms why it's off the table right now. Their understanding will be a great lesson for them and will aid acceptance.
- An old idea that still works: Give your kids a task list and pay them an allowance for completing the list each week, with deductions for tasks not completed. A checklist that they complete and submit can serve as your invoice.
- Share your budget with your kids. Let them see just where the family income goes and how far it goes in a typical month. Wouldn't it have been great if your parents had done that for you?

Assessing the Trend of Your Family's Finances

One of the tools I use in helping businesses to understand their financial situations is to show them two balance sheets—both for the company, but a year apart. For those of you who don't teach business courses, a balance sheet is a financial report that shows all the assets of a company and all its debts or liabilities. The difference between its assets and liabilities is what the company is worth, in theory anyway. So if assets grow but liabilities grow more, or if assets don't grow but liabilities do, the net effect is that the worth of the company gets smaller instead of bigger.

So consider your own balance sheet. You don't have to have a fancy financial report to do this, although Chapter 13 will show you how to get one pretty easily. You just have to have two lists—everything you own and what you think it's worth (your assets), and everything you owe to someone (your liabilities). Subtract the liabilities from the assets, and you've just calculated your estimated net worth. Now do the same thing for a date exactly 12 months earlier and compare the two net-worth numbers. Your worksheet might look like this:

	12/31/2008		12/31/2009
Assets		Assets	
Cash	1,500	Cash	12,600
Cars	35,000	Cars	30,000
Investments	14,600	Investments	9,500
The house	275,000	The house	275,000
Total Assets	326,100	Total Assets	327,100
Liabilities		Liabilities	
Mortgage	246,000	Mortgage	244,000
Credit cards	22,750	Credit cards	36,750
Car loans	15,600	Car loans	14,800
Owed to parents	19,000	Owed to parents	19,000
Total Liabilities	304,350	Total Liabilities	314,550
Net Worth	21,750	Net Worth	12,550

And of course in our example, if the home value went down as well, the picture would look even worse, although not due to spending. So when you did this analysis for yourself, did your net worth get larger or smaller? It's sometimes easy to look at the cash in the bank, see the mortgage getting smaller, and relax about the rest, 'cause it's just life.

But here's what's really happening to our example family: The creditors are slowly beginning to own more of the assets than the family does. If that trend were to continue, their liabilities could soon become larger than their assets, and that has a technical term to describe it. It's called *insolvency,* and it's the first big step toward bankruptcy. Actually, it's the second step. The first step is letting the above example happen to you.

I have learned one important lesson over the years about living with a little less—it was easier when I was younger, and it would be much harder now because I have established a lifestyle that I've become accustomed to. The trick is to become accustomed to a lifestyle that provides not only your immediate needs—although not necessarily all your wants—but also something that will enable you to satisfy more of your needs *and* wants later in life, when you're likely to be less comfortable making sacrifices.

What to Do With That Annual Bonus

While it's far from being a common practice, some school districts actually pay bonuses in addition to salaries. Aside from the efforts by the federal government a few years ago to launch award grants for exceptional performance in low-income areas, some states have adopted the idea that is the cornerstone of motivational reward systems in for-profit companies across the country, a bonus for doing better than expected.

If you are fortunate to have earned a bonus for your work with kids, that's a great opportunity to get a jump on your net-worth-building program by putting the money into an investment instead of a new car or vacation. You've adapted your living standard to your salary, hopefully, so the bonus is really something extra. It's the extra money that is easiest to invest but still tempting to spend. So here's your chance. And don't cheat by using it to make the IRA contribution that you were planning to make anyway out of your salary. Stick with that plan, and make this an additional investment deposit. And if you really can't think of anyplace you want to invest, make a larger payment on your home mortgage, hastening the day when those payments will end and saving some interest in the process.

SUMMARY OF KEY IDEAS FOR CHAPTER 3

1. The best way to handle your paycheck deductions is to try to come out even with the IRS at year-end—you don't owe them, and they don't owe you.

2. Take full advantage of all the opportunities the government offers you for reducing your income taxes—401(k) and IRA plans are all designed to help you keep more of your income so you can have a better future.

3. A traditional IRA will enable you to save taxes today and pay them later when you retire; a Roth IRA will forego today's tax savings for tax-free withdrawals when you retire.

4. Taking a close look at everything you spend money for will likely reveal a host of ways to lower your controllable expenses and provide more money for achieving your goals. You'll be surprised by what you find.

5. You can get a clear picture of how you're doing from one year to the next by creating an annual balance sheet of the family's finances to see how your assets, liabilities, and net worth have changed.

4

Family Finances

Taking Care of the Family's Wish List

Now that you're optimizing the benefits you get from your paycheck, living below your income, and investing your bonus, it's time to think about some of the larger needs of your growing family. If you're planning to have kids—or if that plan is already under way—you'll need to think about college. If you don't plan to have children, that leaves more money for vacations every summer or the backyard pool. If you intend to do all of that, it's time to start planning so the money will be there when you need it, especially if you can get Uncle Sam to help along the way.

College Financial Planning

Some sobering facts: The cost of a private university education today is more than $30,000 a year and climbing. It's more than $13,000 a year for a public university. At commencement time in May 2009, a survey by the National Association of Colleges and Employers indicated just 19.7% of those graduates who applied for a job actually had one.[1] Consider those numbers, and then consider that the competition to get into a good school is greater than ever before. It's easy to understand why having a good education is more important now than ever.

---

1. http://nces.ed.gov/fastfacts/display.asp?id=76

And for most of us, that means lining up some kind of financial assistance to make that education a reality.

Your child's future and the country's economy both are served by the ready availability of more and better educational opportunities. This is dramatically demonstrated whenever unemployment rates rise, as in the recession of 2008–2009. Yet incomes of parents have not kept up with the cost of higher education. No surprise here, but what may be surprising is the incredible range of opportunities for assistance. Whether you consider yourself financially independent or not, it makes sense to explore the many ways your child can get a better education without it all coming out of your pocket.

529 Plans

Nicknamed after the section of the IRS code that gave them life, a 529 savings plan is a tax-advantaged way to save for qualified higher education expenses. Established by almost every state under the IRS permissive regulations, a 529 plan is a little like a beefed-up Roth IRA tailored for postsecondary education. You have to pay federal income taxes on the amounts you contribute to the plan, but earnings on your contribution and subsequent withdrawals are tax free (federal and most states) as long as they're used for qualified educational purposes, whether that means university, community college, or trade school for your child.

Why do this? College is expensive, and some colleges and universities are very expensive. But you already know that. What you may not know: A 2009 survey by Sally Mae, a big student loan provider, reported that some 40% of parents pay no attention to cost when searching for colleges, and 70% of families pay no attention to their child's postgraduation earning potential.[2] Yikes!

Depending on your life plan, the size of your family, and your total earning power by the time your children reach college age, tuition and fees, room and board, and all the rest could become unattainable unless you plan for them well ahead of time. As a result, it makes sense to save in advance as much of the bill as you can before you need to write the check. If your savings can earn something on top of what you put away, that's wonderful. If you can avoid or postpone some income taxes along the way and still get your kids to school, that's best of all.

---

2. *Wall Street Journal*, August 26, 2008, "Best of the Juggle," p. D2.

Your government wants to help. Because college education brings value to the economy as well as to your child and your family, the government is motivated to help you build that college fund in its usual way, with tax savings. These savings plans are among the most widely supported of government programs, as some form of 529 plan is available in every state.

You can contribute to the plan of any state, regardless of where you live, and that might make sense in some cases because of the different characteristics of the state plans. However, it will usually be advantageous to contribute to your state's plan, all other things being equal. For example, most states let you deduct your contributions to their state's plan on your state income taxes, but only three will allow that deduction for some other state's plan. Two states offer a tax credit for contributions to their plan, even more valuable than a tax deduction.[3]

Anyone can contribute to a 529 plan—parents, grandparents, friends, and neighbors. You and your spouse can contribute up to $24,000 a year (or $12,000 per individual), up to a maximum value of $250,000. There is also a provision that allows a lump-sum contribution of $120,000 per married couple or $60,000 per individual. However, many states have lower limits on state income tax deductions they offer for contributions, which is different from the amount of contribution you can legally make to the plan. For example, parents living in Michigan might make a $12,000 contribution to their state plan under IRS regulations, but they will be able to deduct only $5,000 from their state income tax return for that contribution. And by the way, there are some new rules applicable only through 2010 that liberalize what you can do with these plans. As you can see, this is the kind of stuff you want to discuss with your income tax adviser—hopefully a CPA—before you decide.

The substantial limits (compared to IRAs) are in recognition that college expenses are going up every year, and the government wants to foster higher education—don't laugh—by allowing the tax shelter for plan earnings.

As for making sure the money goes for higher education, you control the amount contributed, including where the funds get invested, so the kids can't use it to buy themselves new cars for the prom. If Bud decides he doesn't want to go to college in spite of the 529 funds awaiting him, you can divert the funds to Bud's sister Mary, who wants to go to Yale but doesn't have enough 529 money to cover it. Also there are penalties for not using the money for education—including paying federal income taxes on earnings withdrawn plus a

---

3. http://www.savingforcollege.com/bankrate_articles/article.php?article_id=45

10% penalty for not using it for the intended purpose. (The original contribution is not taxed since you already paid tax on that when you made the contribution.)

Having said all this about tax benefits and penalties, I have to tell you I'm not a tax expert (you'll get that caveat again when you get to Chapter 12), and I don't keep up with all the tax rule changes. So at the risk of overstating the obvious, please consult with your tax adviser before you take steps to set up a 529 plan. However, as a starting point, know that there are two flavors of plans with some significant differences between them. They are classified as either *college savings plans* or *prepaid tuition plans*. In general, a college savings plan lets you save and invest for the college years and then spend that money on most of the significant costs your child will incur in going to school, at whatever those things cost at the time. A prepaid tuition plan, by contrast, gives you the opportunity to prepay tuition and fees (only) at selected schools and lock in the current rates regardless of what happens to those rates by the time your child actually gets to school. These prepaid plans can eliminate a lot of uncertainty about future costs, but you may find the range of schools that offer them limited to mostly state schools.

There are a lot of exceptions and more subtle differences that you'll find once you start digging into it. You can find an excellent introduction to these plans, along with a table of comparisons between the two types of plans at www.sec.gov/investor/pubs/intro529.htm.

One final thought: If you already have a 529 plan and the investment meltdown of 2008–2009 took a bite out of your college fund, don't automatically pull your money out of the plan and stick it under the mattress. Read the investment ideas in Chapters 9 and 10 before you make any decisions. You may want to consider simply moving your funds to a different 529 plan that invests more conservatively. However, if your child has more than a few years before starting college, you have time to recoup much of your losses through the normal recovery of the markets, as long as you are invested in basically sound funds to begin with.

Scholarships and Grants

While I do not consider myself qualified to consult on scholarships (I turned down the only scholarship offer I got so I could go to a school near home instead of one halfway across the country), this book would not be complete without some information to start parents of college-bound children in the right direction for this valuable source of financial assistance. There are a host of web resources you can use in your search for scholarships and grants. I checked out www.scholarshipproviders.org as the most credible association of grantors and www.collegescholarships.org for tons of details about the kinds of grant programs available. Here's the minimum you should know before you start shopping.

Scholarships: Awards for Merit

Scholarships are not just for scholarship anymore. The challenge in getting a college education these days has not escaped many organizations that want to support people like themselves or people who have similar interests. That's not to say that your child can earn a scholarship by being a poor student, because performance in school is always a criterion when there are more applicants than available funds (which is to say always), but there are ways to narrow the field by finding foundations and funding organizations with special interests or concerns that other applicants don't have.

Types of Scholarships

Degree Specific. Mostly we hear about scholarships available for undergrads, the high school kids wanting to get to college. And in truth those are the most numerous in availability from countless sources. But there are also scholarships available for degreed students seeking advanced degrees, including masters and doctorates. It pays to shop around for these, because few sources offer help at all three levels.

Career Specific. There are scholarships specifically intended to support your child's interest in a particular career, made available because someone or some organization wants to encourage students to pursue that course of study. Included in current offerings are engineering, math and science, the information technology fields, business, history, journalism, psychology, and even library science.

Athletic. Earmarked for the premier athletes in high schools across the country, these are always competitive, often pitting 10 candidates in competition for a single position on the team (and a single scholarship). An athlete must move quickly to accept one if offered before another student snaps it up. Of course if your child is superstar material, schools have been known to juggle scholarships among positions to make sure that superstar doesn't get away, but don't count on that happening with any regularity. Division 1 schools all have scholarship money, as do some Division 2 schools. Division 3 schools will not have money for scholarships. That said, it's still good to keep in mind that there may be less competition at the smaller schools, some of which might be willing to provide an education in return for playing for the school.

Minority. Young white males are about the only kind of student who won't find some agency, corporate donor, university, or other kind of organization offering scholarship money specifically because of their ethnicity. If your child fits into one of the other categories, be sure to explore these options, especially if they plan to pursue study in underrepresented fields, such as the sciences, math, engineering, technical subjects, law, medicine, and business. There are even scholarships for interracial or multicultural students who don't feel they fit neatly into one racial or cultural background.

Political or Religious Organizations. Not to mix the two, but both these groups have influence and money and a strong interest in educating their young people (and keeping them connected to the cause). If you have a strong connection to one of these organizations, explore their interest in educational support. And if your child is interested in theological studies in any of the major religions, contact your church, school, or temple to find out how they can help.

Student Activities Support. If your child was active in the Boy Scouts or Girl Scouts, or in political activities, or is a web designer, or a vegan, there may be scholarship money available because of that activity. If you recall the role that blogging played in the election of Barack Obama, it won't surprise you to know there are scholarships available in political blogging. It may surprise you, though, to learn that your daughter, the beauty pageant contestant, may be able to get scholarship help from Miss America and several other pageant organizations.

Nontraditional Schools. If your child attended a vocational school or technical school, or even if your child was homeschooled, there may be financial help specifically for him or her.

Grants: A Gift of Education

Unlike scholarships that are awarded primarily based on merit, grants are most often based on financial need. In addition, grants do not need to be repaid; they are free gifts to the student wishing to pursue a higher education. The U.S. government and many organizations that grant scholarships also provide outright grants to students who, while perhaps not able to qualify for a scholarship, still would benefit from a college education.

The U.S. government may be the largest source of educational grants, but it is by no means the only source. People serving in the military have long had the opportunity to get a partially or fully paid college education as part of the armed forces' efforts to produce officers for the various services. Today those services offer grants to spouses of active-duty personnel as well. The variety and type of organizations offering grants is virtually as unlimited as with scholarships, and not all of them require demonstration of financial need. Many are from colleges that simply want to attract good students to their campuses.

While most grants are simple gifts, some grants require a service in return for the grant, such as a year or two in an underserved medical or educational institution. My service in the Navy ROTC program while in school entitled me to supplemental funds from the Navy in return for my commitment to serve on active duty after graduation.

One well-known grant opportunity offered by the U.S. government is called the Pell Grant, named after the senator who sponsored the enabling legislation in 1972. Designed to enable low-income students to get valuable education beyond high school, these grants are for the most part out of reach of most teachers, since the average household income to qualify is in the range of $20,000.

At the other end of the grant spectrum from those in need are grants for postgraduate and doctoral candidates. Many types of grant programs are available to advanced students from colleges, universities, and private organizations. Colleges and universities are quite competitive in offering grant awards to the right candidates, and in some instances, grants may support most of a doctoral student's research and living expenses.

Grad students who must travel to participate in studies abroad, take part in research, or attend professional conferences may discover a slew of small grants administered by professional organizations or college travel grants designed to cover such auxiliary expenses.

Loan Programs

When your child cannot qualify for a scholarship, and your income is too high to enable him or her to obtain a grant, there are always a host of loan programs available. Probably the best source of information on these programs is the government-agency-turned-private-corporation known as Sally Mae. The company primarily provides federal and private student loans for undergraduate and graduate students and their parents. Sally Mae is also, according to its website,[4] "the nation's leading provider of student loans and administrator of college savings plans."

---

4. http://www.salliemae.com/about

The federal government is the largest source of student loans in the country, funding over $100 billion annually. Some readers may already be familiar with such programs, including the Teacher Education Assistance for College and Higher Education (TEACH) Grant Program that provides grants of up to $4,000 per year to students who intend to teach in schools serving students from low-income families.

The good thing about student loans—they are widely available to most everyone who wants to go to college, usually at very favorable interest rates. The downside is that they have to be repaid after graduation, when they loom large to the new graduate trying to establish a new life outside the parents' domain. Happily, there are a wide variety of repayment options available from the federal government's loan programs and even a loan forgiveness program for those interested in public service jobs.[5]

Not to stop there, Uncle Sam has recently added an online tool to help you determine eligibility for various federal aid programs and to point you in the right direction. The tool, called FAFSA4caster, available at http://studentaid.ed.gov, enables students considering furthering their education beyond high school to calculate their eligibility for federal financial aid, including grants, and reduce the time it will take to complete the application.

Despite the huge amounts of aid provided by the government, U.S. Department of Education student aid is not the only source of such aid, and federal aid maximums have not kept up with tuition increases over the past few years. Nonfederal financial assistance programs and requirements often vary from school to school, but you'll have to contact the schools directly for their details.

Beyond the schools, many financial companies offer student loans as well to fill the gap beyond the dollar limits set by federal programs and to establish customer relationships with graduates, who are likely to become financially well off in the future. Internet search terms like *college loan programs* will bring up a seemingly endless list of them. Terms are not as flexible, interest rates are not likely to be as low, and many financial institutions have tightened lending standards in this area as with other kinds of lending. Still, there are lots of competitors to compare. The thing to keep in mind is that, while government sites are dry, dull, and information only, private company sites are commercials for their lending services. So don't take every statement the financial companies make at face value without checking them out carefully. Do your homework. It's good practice for the rest of your financial life.

---

5. http://studentaid.ed.gov

College Entrance Tutoring

Being in the education business, you may already know that high school counselors are typically overworked and underinformed, while the number of applicants to less costly public universities is climbing. So it's only natural that someone would fill the void and come up with an idea to help the kids and their families beyond the support that the school system is able to provide. And as it turns out, the range of services is all over the map, from content tutoring in specific topics or guidance in filling out the application all the way to intensive multiyear coaching on such wide-ranging areas of assistance as the following:

- Building a resume that will be appealing to admissions officers
- Visiting and selecting the school or schools that will be applied to and gearing coaching to the specific requirements of desired schools
- Getting involved in extracurricular activities that broaden your child's awareness as well as appeal to admissions officers
- Overcoming intimidation at the prospect of applying
- Coaching the parents in how best to support their child's aspirations
- Writing a high-quality application to any number of schools
- Coaching your child through challenges while in school or when he or she begins planning what comes after college graduation

These coaching services, like any other professional service, are only as good as the counselors you work with, so selecting a service and a counselor are key decisions for a parent. With that thought in mind, the biggest firm in the business is not as important as getting a qualified, caring counselor. The best of these services are selective in choosing who they work with, and you should be too.

A small business client of mine, College Launch LLC, in Pasadena, California, is a good example of the wide range of services that can be offered to help your child get prepared for college. They address the myriad challenges involved in preparing for, applying to, getting accepted to, and succeeding at the college of one's choice, sometimes starting the grooming process as early as middle school. It seems the really good schools don't just want studious applicants anymore; they want well-rounded, young citizens. The College Launch website speaks not just of entrance exam tutoring or application writing but of services that "address a student's academic IQ needs by developing their emotional quotient (EQ) in a nurturing, social environment, while engaging the support and understanding of the whole family."[6]

---

6. http://www.collegelaunch.com/services.html

As for the cost of such broad assistance, fees vary widely for these services, so it pays to shop around. But just like a company trying to hire a good employee, it's better to screen the service for the quality and nature of what it offers and then select the best fee structure from among qualified providers. Also it's a good idea to ask your friends if they've used a service that they really liked. Their experience will help you decide on the intangibles. Shopping for price first could get you into a really cheap service offering that gives you less than you paid for and costs you precious time besides. And when you finally choose a firm, don't be afraid to negotiate for a lower fee or a payment plan or both.

Life Insurance for the Kids?

At some point along the way, someone is going to offer you the opportunity to buy life insurance on the lives of your infants or young children. These are typically very small policies of whole life insurance[7] at small premiums, the idea being to lock in a cheap rate and give your children a start in buying insurance for themselves later on. I bought such a policy for my young son, and in retrospect, I have to ask myself why. It didn't have anything to do with my later choices in insurance; my son cashed the policy in almost as soon as I gave it to him.

I don't think anything changed as a result of my purchase, except that I paid premiums for 15 years or so for an insurance policy that paid someone commissions for selling me something we didn't need. My apologies to your uncle who sells insurance—as mine did. Insurance is a long-term commitment of financial resources as a protection against financial difficulties. It is not an expression of love or joy about your newborn son or daughter, nor is refusing to provide that insurance any statement about you or your child. It's a financial purchase. If you think the protection will be valuable to your child down the road, then by all means do it. If I had to do it again, I would not; that's all.

Vacation Financing

Ah, vacations. They are wonderful escapes from the everyday demands of life, at least for a week or two. How wonderful it is depends in large measure on our state of mind and also on how many pleasurable experiences we can build into those 14 days. And that often translates into how much money we can afford to spend. In recent years, it wasn't hard to find a TV commercial in which some bank offered to finance your

---

7. Refer to Chapter 6 for a more thorough discussion of insurance.

next dream vacation with a loan backed by the equity in your house. Well, those days are gone for the time being, so you'll actually get to make a decision about this without the influence of Countrywide or WeMakeItEasy.com to coax you into borrowing on the house.

From Debt or Savings?

> ⌐° **KEY POINT**
>
> So what's the best way to finance a vacation? Out of your income. What does that mean for the years when you have a small income? You have a small vacation.

If that seems to be an unsympathetic stance (even when you consider that this is a book about financial management), let's take a more helpful look at how you might do that.

Consider building a vacation fund. When I was a kid, the nation's savings and loans collected deposits from their customers with campaigns called Christmas clubs or vacation clubs. They helped us put aside small amounts of money each month, for which they paid us a ridiculously low rate of interest, in return for which they sent us a nice check just in time to spend it on gifts for the family or that summer vacation. That old-fashioned idea has long since died, but the concept is much easier to do for yourself these days. If you set up an automatic funds transfer with your bank, you can create your own vacation club. The interest you'll earn is probably close to what we earned when I was a kid, but the point isn't income; it's a forced savings plan for something you really want—a getaway in the summer.

So how much to put aside? If you think of a modest vacation trip for 12 or 13 days for you and your spouse, your expense might look like this:

Airfare via coach on LowCostAir or driving cost for 1,600 miles round trip in the family car	$800
Hotel for 12 nights at $100 a night	$1,200
Shopping or eating out money at $100 a day	$1,200
Mad money—for that dress or tennis racquet you or your spouse just have to get right now	$200
Total cost for the trip	$3,400

If you save for 11 months and spend it all in the 12th month, that's a monthly saving of $310 a month, or $155 a month from each of your salaries. If you want to test some of your numbers to see what the monthly savings would have to be, there's a model for that at www

.corwin.com/financialmastery. If you are single and plan to stay that way at least through the vacation, the airfare and eating out money will be perhaps $1,000 less (and you don't have to wrangle over who gets to spend the mad money), and the monthly nut would be $218, since you can't rent half a room. That's a fairly sizeable monthly investment that you might gladly make for that summer escape. And of course if you have kids that will come along, the numbers get even bigger. But how might you get the cost down without sacrificing too much of the experience?

More Vacation for Less Money

Here are a few ideas for stretching your vacation dollars without having to live on fast-food cheeseburgers to pay for it.

1. **Buy two time-share vacation weeks.** A vacation week at a condo-style time-share resort can be bought on the pre-owned market for as little as $1,000[8] or as much as $5,000 and up, depending on where it is and what time of year your week is. This is a full week at a very nice destination that you purchase and own for as long as you choose to, with only a modest annual maintenance fee paid to the homeowners' association thereafter.

Explore the options at www.redweek.com, and learn about time-share vacations at the same time. Membership at this independent site is currently $14.99 a year, and they have lots of educational information, resort reviews, and a searchable bulletin board where time-share owners post their weeks for sale or rental at prime resorts around the world, often for a fraction of what the daily rental would be at that resort or a comparable hotel.

With a time payment plan for your time-share, your annual cost for a 2-week vacation at a five-star resort, which otherwise rents for $250 to $300 a night, instead of the $100 in my hotel example, could look like this:

Airfare via coach on LowCostAir or driving cost for 1,600 miles round trip in the family car	$800
Annual maintenance fee to the resort association	$500
Shopping or eating out money at $100 a day	$1,200
Mad money—for that dress or tennis racquet you or your spouse just have to get right now	$200
Total cost for the trip	$2,700

8. Breezy Point Timeshare, Pequot Lakes, Minnesota (http://www.redweek.com/resort/P1727-breezy-point-timeshare).

That's quite a difference—saving that much over 11 months would require a put aside of $245 a month, but only after the time-share purchase is paid off, perhaps 3 or 4 years down the road. Time-share purchases are easily financed over 3 to 5 years, making their payments probably less than your daily Starbucks purchase. After that, you will own 2 weeks at that resort, and you'll own them forever, until you choose to sell them.

Resale weeks are not like real estate in the normal sense. They don't really appreciate in value, and if you buy a week from the resort itself, you will likely pay more for it than you can sell it for later. But in the secondary market—buying from other time-share owners— you will likely get a price which, based on the last 10 years of history, could be pretty close to what you paid for it.

Join RedWeek.com or an exchange club, and for another $300 a year, you can trade your week at one resort for a different week at any of a hundred other resorts around the world, subject to availability. We have several time-share weeks, and I'm convinced this is the most inexpensive way to have a really nice vacation—unless, for you, a really nice vacation involves expensive plane tickets, which aren't included. In addition, I used some of our time-share weeks to write this book, since a resort is a pretty nice place to work in isolation for a creative project or a time-sensitive one.

2. **Partner with another couple and share the cost.** If you have friends that you enjoy being with—for a week or two, that is, not just an evening—consider planning your vacation together and sharing the cost of such things as housing, car travel expenses, and so forth. The savings you'll realize will depend on the kind of vacation you are planning, but it will be less than if you go it alone, to be sure. If you both have children, the savings could add up to half your housing bill, as the kids would probably love to share a room without the parents around. OK, maybe that's not always a good idea, but it's a thought. Disclaimer: I was not paid by your kids to say that.

3. **Have a grander vacation every other year.** Perhaps one year is a continuing education summer, and the next year is a vacation that would cost you more than you might otherwise spend, but you'd have two years to save up for it. This doesn't sound like as much fun as having an annual vacation, but it's a good way to have a vacation and not have to think, "How can I do this cheaper," with every planned activity. The memories are fewer in the early years but richer. I did this when I was younger and had a naval reserve obligation to fulfill. I would use my vacation time every other year to fulfill my

military duty and save the money I earned for a more enchanting vacation the following year. Looking back on it now, I don't remember the years I skipped, but I fondly remember the vacations.

4. Tour group vacations. I'm sure you know even more about tour group travel than I do, so I'll only mention it here. Group travel is less expensive than individual travel, and you'll have a professional travel planner laying out the trip, which likely means you'll get to see things you might not if you had planned it in your spare time. I've spoken to tour company audiences before, and they're pretty serious about creating great experiences for their customers. Group travel leaves more money to add a purse and shoes to that dress or some professional lessons to accompany the tennis racquet.

5. Borrow the money to have a grand vacation every year. Just kidding. It is never a good idea to borrow money to spend on a vacation, other than small credit card purchases that you intend to pay off when the statement arrives. The term *mortgaging your future* really comes to life if you spend borrowed money on entertainment and travel from which there is nothing tangible remaining after you unpack. Borrow for a house, yes; for a car, yes; for a good time, maybe not.

SUMMARY OF KEY IDEAS FOR CHAPTER 4

1. The cost of a 4-year college education today can easily exceed 2 years of your salary. If you want your kids to get the education you got or better, you must seriously plan ahead for it and save for it.

2. A 529 plan is the best way to use federal tax laws to support your children's college funds. Happily, there's a plan somewhere that suits your needs if you'll just look for it.

3. If your child is smart or particularly talented, there is probably scholarship money available to him or her. If he or she isn't but still wants that diploma, grants and loans are even more plentiful, but not without some effort to qualify for them.

4. Vacations are great; often they come with a financial hangover if you're not careful. Well-planned vacations with your budget in mind are great with no ill effects afterward. You don't have to give up vacations to build a nice financial future.

5

Managing Debt

When You Have Too
Much of a Good Thing

To paraphrase Gordon Gekko, "Debt is good." But just as in the classic 1987 film about Wall Street, it's the context that's important. Uncontrolled greed is destructive, as the characters in the film ultimately learned and as Wall Street learned for real in 2008. Uncontrolled debt is equally destructive. The ease with which millions of Americans have accumulated debt has finally led to record numbers of bankruptcies, a condition that exists as this book is written and is expected to continue for some time into the future.

It is far too easy to believe it's all right to consume today and pay for it tomorrow, and there are actually very few instances when that is true. In fact, I suggest to you that the only occasions when debt is financially sensible are these:

- Buying something that will last a long time, and stretching the payments for it over the period in which you get value—your house and your car are good examples
- Making an investment where the proceeds are expected to pay for the initial outlay as well as repayment of the debt and deliver a profit besides
- Taking out a student loan to pay for your college education, not at the most expensive school you can get into, but one that will launch you properly into your career

- Using debt to level out a standard of living where income fluctuates from high to low, and you want to avoid having such fluctuations in your lifestyle

I added that last one with some trepidation because of the difficulty we frequently encounter in matching the highs of our spending with the highs of our income, usually by overspending and underearning. In any event, it's a valid option for the sales professional spouse, for example, who has short periods of low sales followed by periods of high sales.

The problem arises when debt gets out of hand and becomes unmanageable. The guy who has to have a new car every other year, or who leases his cars because "the payments are lower," doesn't really use up the value he has paid for before he begins paying for it again. The woman who has to have the latest wardrobe for her professional appearance and postpones savings for later is betting that later will be much better than today—think Sarah Jessica Parker in *Sex and the City*—not usually a safe bet. The family who repeatedly trades up their home, always investing any increase in value in a larger down payment on the next home, is not building wealth until the family stays in one place long enough for value increases to catch up. And the sales professional who has more down periods than up periods but keeps spending like the good times are right around the corner is likely to find something else around the corner. These and other examples of bad debt can be thought of as things that improve your lifestyle only temporarily.

But then sometimes we just learn by experience, and when that happens, we need to work our way out and make sure we get the lesson. This chapter is intended to help you learn more quickly and with less pain.

Debt Can Stress Your Marriage to the Breaking Point

There are few things more consistently on the list of marriage breakups than money—maybe in-laws, but that's it. Money, or the lack of it, is a great stress creator, and too much debt speaks loudly of the lack of money. Thus debt becomes the devil, and the relationship gets lost in the details. It's not that debt is so bad by itself (remember, "debt is good"), it's that couples have different fears around debt and different risk tolerances around uncertainty. If those differences didn't get surfaced and dealt with before the marriage, it's a certainty they will come up to be addressed during the marriage. So here are some ideas for getting those differences merged into a compromise policy you can both live with and love with.

1. Develop a common philosophy on debt that you will both follow, addressing issues like the following:
   a. Will we pay cash for things we buy every day or charge things to a credit card?
   b. Will we pay off all our credit card balances every month, or are we comfortable carrying a balance? And if a balance is OK, how much?
   c. Will we spend only up to the amount of our current income, or can we occasionally overspend for a special purchase? If we allow the occasional overspend, how soon must we be able to pay it off?
   d. Will our savings accounts be off limits to spending except in emergencies, or are there other things we can dip into it for, such as a vacation?
   e. What is our definition of an emergency expense?

2. Decide where debt and savings stand on your priority list. Will you pay off all debts before starting to save or stretch the debt repayment to start building savings sooner?

3. If either of you had debts from before the marriage that are still unpaid, is that the original debtor's responsibility to pay off, or will you pay it off out of the family's joint income?

If you ask these questions together, you *will* find differences; I guarantee it. The key is reaching a compromise that both of you can live with and not be irritated every time it comes up. For example, suppose the wife wants to ensure savings are used only for emergencies, period. The husband thinks that is much too severe a rule and wants more flexibility, such as for the annual family vacation. Perhaps a compromise might be that we will try to finance our vacation out of our income, but we can tap savings for up to $1,000 if needed. An excellent book on this whole subject is *Financially Ever After* by Jeff D. Opdyke,[1] from which some of these ideas were adapted.

If you are not married but intend to be in the future, you have a rare opportunity to do this the easy way instead of the hard way. Have this discussion in the same way you'll have that talk about how

---

1. *Financially Ever After*, Jeff D. Opdyke, published by Collins Business, 2009.

many kids you want to have, where your first home will be (your place or mine or a new one), and who gets to drive the new car.

Credit Cards: Huge Differences Exist Just Beneath the Surface

Everybody needs a credit card these days, for online purchases, airline and rental car reservations, and more. In appearance, they all are exactly alike. They're the same size with pictures and numbers on one side and a magnetic strip and your signature on the other side. That's where the similarities end.

Credit cards are vastly different in the ways they charge you for using them and the terms and conditions that they require. Most of those terms and conditions would, if the banks issuing the cards were unchallenged, be hidden under the magnetic strip so you could never see them until your interest rate suddenly doubled. OK, perhaps I exaggerate. But the point is there are some requirements for using a credit card that make one card much more expensive for you or less valuable to use or both. Which card is best for you depends on the way you use it.

As this was written, the federal government had just passed the Credit Card Act of 2009, historic legislation to severely limit the ways in which credit card issuers can take advantage of you, to the credit of President Obama and Congress. If you've had a credit card for a while, even as a student, you may have personally experienced some of the abuses this new law will curb. Some of those changes include the following:

- No more retroactive interest rate increases are applied because you missed a payment date.
- You get at least 21 days after the bill is mailed to pay your bill each month before the payment is late.
- You receive 45 days' advance notice of changes in terms of use, penalties, late charges, and so forth.
- Payments beyond the minimum amount must be applied to the highest interest rate balance first.
- Here's a good one: The bank must tell you how long it will take to pay off the balance if you make only the minimum payment each month.
- There's more, but you get the idea.

Not to be undone, issuing banks were quick to move to protect their most profitable product. Rapid increases followed for a range of fees and interest rates, sometimes dramatically, to slip in under the wire of the new law. Here are some examples just in overdraft fees that you might not be aware of:

1. If you use a debit card and exceed your cash balance, your bank may pay the charge anyway then charge you an overdraft fee. One source estimates debit cards trigger 46% of all overdrafts.[2] The fix: Have your bank set your debit card overdraw amount to zero.

2. If you don't pay your overdraft fees promptly, some banks will quickly add still more fees; one adds $35 after 7 days. The fix: Arrange an automatic line of credit or transfer from your savings account to back up your checking account.

3. If you actually do overdraw on your account, some banks don't reject anything until the item count gets pretty high, charging you for every one, and in some cases, the amount of the fee increases with each new overdraft. The fix: Don't be reticent about asking the bank to reverse those extra fees. If it's a rare occurrence in your account, they should agree.

Still, if you are committed to paying your balance off every month as soon as the statement arrives, the fact that the card charges 28% on unpaid balances doesn't matter. That is, unless the interest charges begin as soon as the charge is posted to your account, days or even weeks before you see the statement, which is often the case. And frequent flyer miles for what you spend may be worth a lot to you, unless your spouse works for an airline that lets you travel anytime you want, or you travel only once or twice a year. And cash discounts on what you buy may bring you solid cash refunds periodically, unless they give discounts only on goods and services you never buy. And interest-free balance transfers from another card may not be worth much if the rate goes up 4 months later to the aforementioned 28%.

Twenty-eight percent? "Can they actually get that high," you might ask, and the answer is, "Yes!" Some cards can get into the 30s, even today. No one in Washington has required banks to lower their interest charges on credit cards just because there's been a recession, and so far few banks have volunteered to do that. Since credit cards are invariably their most profitable product, even after the collection losses the media write about, banks are not particularly motivated to

---

2. Center for Responsible Lending, as reported in *Wall Street Journal*, August 21, 2008, "Some Tips for Avoiding Pricey Overdraft Fees," p. D2.

cut their revenue, as you can imagine. The new law will certainly change the balance somewhat, but as noted, banks have been quick to add additional fees to try to make up the difference. In addition, collection efforts on delinquent accounts have become more aggressive, so it's best to carry credit card balances only as a temporary, emergency source of funds.

The point of all this is that you need to shop around and avoid signing up for the first card offer that arrives in your mailbox, promising instant approval and free doughnuts. The features that banks use to attract you to their cards are truly creative, both for your benefit and theirs if you get the right one. So here are some thoughts and ideas to consider when shopping for a new credit card.

Shopping on the Web

I can't think of anywhere the Web has become more valuable to you and me than in shopping for credit among competing lenders. And believe me when I tell you there are a truly wide variety of choices with a wide variety of costs associated with those choices in the form of interest rates (teaser, permanent, and contingent), fees, credit limits, and of course, benefits. Without leaving your living room, you can find banks willing to consider you for a credit card if you want balance-transfer cards, low-interest-rate cards, instant-approval cards, and no-credit-history cards. You can find a card designed just for you if you have excellent, weak, or even bad credit. If you have a bankruptcy on your record, you can still get a prepaid card that acts like a credit card but is supported by, and limited by, the amount of cash you have on deposit at the issuing bank. Oh, and don't confuse these prepaid cards with debit cards—discussed later in the chapter—where you have ready access to your money.

Rewards are offered for so many categories of use that you can pretty much pick the card that rewards you with cash or points or miles for whatever kind of spending pattern you have. You can even get a credit card with pictures of your family on it, if that's what you want. Of course there are trade-offs for all these great benefits. The sweeter the rewards, the higher the interest rates, annual fees, over-limit charges, and so forth.

You can compare credit card offers from several banks to see which one is best for you. Some places to check out include www.bankrate.com, www.creditcards.com, www.creditcardguide .com, or www.creditcardmenu.com for this kind of information. For example, creditcards.com offers 14 banks that will consider issuing a card to people who admit up front to having bad credit. Some of those are prepaid or secured cards, but they look pretty much like a regular credit card as long as you stay within the limit of the cash you have put up as security for your credit line. Just keep in mind that these websites are not your trusted financial adviser. They get paid by the credit card companies to send them new prospective cardholders. I thought about inserting a table into the book to show you the choices that are available, but it would never fit on a page, or several pages, for that matter, so you'll just have to go shopping for yourself.

My recommendations for using credit cards include the following:

1. Accept that owning a credit card or two is necessary in our economy in order to establish a credit history for yourself. If you ever want to buy a car or a house, you'll need that credit history to exist, and to look good financially, in order to get a loan.

2. Don't own more cards than you need. One or two should be enough for most of us. We think we're privileged when we get still another offer to extend $5,000 or $10,000 in easy credit, but that's just a recipe for getting into financial trouble. When things get tight, we're tempted to use all that credit, and that's when the real trouble starts. It's important that you have credit available when you need it. It's equally important that you use that capability with care and caution.

3. If you have a good credit record, you should not have to accept interest rates greater than 12% to 15% on carried balances. Depending on the credit environment, you might be able to get a balance transfer card that will offer you a single-digit interest rate on a balance transferred for as long as it takes you to pay off that balance. As this book was written, payments on such balances have traditionally been applied in a way that costs you the greatest amount of interest over the repayment period. But the Credit Card Act of 2009 changed all that, as noted previously. As of February 2010, any monthly payment amounts in excess of the minimum payment due *must* be applied to balances with the highest interest rate first, and then to balances with the next highest rate, and so on.

4. If you have gotten in too far—your balance is too high, or your interest rate is too high, or both—consider calling the credit card company and asking for relief. Considerable energy was devoted to helping struggling cardholders during the 2008–2009 recession, and banks were encouraging cardholders to call and work something out rather than just stop paying on the balance.

Credit Cards Versus Charge Cards

These sound similar, but they're really quite different. We've been talking about credit cards up to this point in this chapter. You buy something and charge it. The issuing bank pays the merchant and then sends you a bill for the charge, plus interest, for you to pay the bank back. You can pay them in full when you get the bill, or you can pay them a minimum monthly payment for months into the distant future, at your option.

A charge card, by contrast, requires you to pay the bank back in full when you get the statement. American Express cards have worked like this for years (although they now also offer credit cards that have some of the bells and whistles of other cards, including time payments and interest charges). The American Express green and gold cards charge no interest if you pay the balance promptly, and there is no provision in their terms for time payments. So they're charge cards, not credit cards, in the sense that they won't lend you the balance due for any longer than it takes them to send you a monthly statement. The value of a charge card is that you know you have to pay it off promptly, so you have no balance to build up, no interest charges, and no getting out of control. The only downside is that they typically have a very large amount that you can charge on the card in any one month, so you still have to be careful.

Debit Cards: A Safer Idea

As most everyone knows by now, a debit card looks very much like a credit card, but it's connected to your checking account, and your checking account is effectively the collateral for your purchases. You buy something, use your debit card to pay for it, and the money comes directly out of your bank account in the next few days. The charge shows up on your monthly bank statement just like a check. There are no separate credit card statements and no interest charges, because you're spending your own money, not the bank's money. So there are no late charges, no interest charges, no over-limit charges, and no balance buildup. Consider using your debit card instead of your credit card for most purchases. You don't borrow, so you don't have to repay, much safer as a personal financial strategy.

Getting Help Before It's Too Late: Debt Counseling Services

When I started my consulting practice over 20 years ago, it was not under optimum conditions. I had no clients, no network of contacts who would refer clients, and not much capital to hold me over until I got clients. As I went deeper in debt supporting myself, I was sure I was smart enough in finance to take care of myself, so I didn't ask for help from anyone. I managed for a couple of years with expense greater than my income while I built that network, signed my first clients, and became financially viable. By then I had a mountain of credit card debt that would take many years to repay. I suspect a credit counselor would have given me some tips that I wasn't smart enough to give myself during those years, such as, "Spend less. Market better. Work faster. Live on a budget!" I don't know what the advice would have been, and that's the point. The end result for me was a personal bankruptcy. I got a fresh start, but my way of doing it has always bothered me. It's the one thing I know I would do differently if I had the chance.

Sometimes we just get in over our heads.

And that's what debt counseling services are for—to help us think and act clearly when we don't have a clear plan or when we're trying to hide our dilemma or when we're just scared. If you Google "debt counseling services," you will get a plethora of choices in service offerings, some free, some not. The best place to go in order to choose a reputable counseling firm to work with is the National Foundation for Credit Counseling (NFCC) website (www.nfcc.org). They maintain membership requirements, they certify firms in their ethics, methods, and practices, and they provide a wealth of educational materials to individuals and counselors on managing money, debt relief, bankruptcy processes, and more. You can also find a government-approved counseling service from the U.S. Department of Justice at www.usdoj.gov/ust/, although their list of services, as of April 2009, hadn't been updated since 2006, so be prepared to find out that some of them are no longer in business.

At NFCC's website you can get guidance on getting out of debt completely, if that's your goal, or simply get information about managing it better or buy publications to guide your credit counseling choices.

Remember: You are entitled to get one free copy of your credit report from each of the three principal reporting agencies once a year.

You should take advantage of that every year, so you know what others are seeing. The place to go is www.annualcreditreport.com. One caveat: your mortgage lender uses a slightly different scoring system, so your credit score will be different in their eyes, often lower, than in the reports you see.

SUMMARY OF KEY IDEAS FOR CHAPTER 5

1. Uncontrolled debt by both consumers and corporations created the financial crisis of 2008–2009. Still, debt is a good thing, provided it's used for

   a. an affordable house or car,

   b. a good investment,

   c. a student loan to ensure your child gets a college education,

   d. a *temporary* means to level out manageable swings in income.

2. Every couple must establish early in their marriage (or even sooner) how they will handle debt—incurring it, repaying it—including compromise commitments where values differ.

3. Credit cards are the blessing and curse of consumer credit. The blessing is they are easy to use. The curse is they are easy to use. As a result, more consumers are driven to bankruptcy through out-of-control credit card debt than by home foreclosures.

4. Use a charge card or debit card in preference to a credit card. They're safer and less expensive.

5. Debt counseling services are not just for poor debtors; they're for anyone who can't manage his or her debts but really wants to.

6

Insurance

Just in Case

In the early days of this country, when we were mostly a land of rural communities, there was a common practice that occurred if your house burned down or got destroyed by some other act of nature. Your neighbors would come around and help you rebuild it—without charge, even contributing whatever materials were needed for the construction process. They did that readily because they were your neighbors and because they knew that in the same situation, you would do the same for them. Catastrophe insurance was in effect provided by the community, which shared the risk of loss for any one neighbor and thus for all.

That wouldn't work today for lots of reasons. One of them: I don't even know my neighbors two doors down the street, and I don't ever drop over for tea or bring a cake to the community festival that we don't have. My guess is that many of you are in the same boat with your neighbors, so we need someone to help rebuild the house or repair our damaged car or whatever. Insurance companies arose to fill that need, collecting small amounts of resources—insurance premiums instead of wooden planks—from all the "neighbors" and using it to help the one with the problem to rebuild. The insurance company tried to guess how many houses they'd have to rebuild and what that would cost. Then they divided that cost by the number of policyholders (community members) they had and sent each an invoice for his or her fair share—plus a modest profit, of course. They invested the money until they needed it, and their investment returns helped to lower the amount of each community member's resource contribution.

Today it works pretty much the same way, except for the modest part. You can get insurance for just about anything if you're willing to pay the premium. On the flip side, insurance companies will sometimes decide the numbers don't work out for them, and they'll announce that they'll no longer rebuild the neighbor's house in California or Florida, or they'll no longer accept no-fault auto insurance policyholders, or whatever. Still, the system works most of the time, and happily, the kinds of insurance that we need most—those that insure our lives and health—are offered by lots of companies. This chapter provides some of the basic facts and perhaps a caveat or two about each of them. If I've left your favorite insurance off the list, apologies in advance. And since this is such brief coverage of such a broad topic, please consult your insurance adviser for the many details I have left out before making a decision.

Life Insurance

Since life can only be insured, not ensured, life insurance is really more like a reward to the survivors when someone dies. If you live long enough to outlast anyone who has made you the beneficiary of his or her policy, you could be richly rewarded indeed. That is, of course, if the insurance company they paid their premiums to is still around to pay your claim. Thus the health of the company is just as important as the health of the insured person, except that it's easier to find out.

Just as we all have credit scores and grades to evaluate our standing in society, all provided by some independent, supposedly objective overseer, insurance companies have an overseer too. A. M. Best is the company that provides health ratings on insurance companies. Insurers refer to their A. M. Best rating whenever it's good enough to brag about, and they're very quiet when it's not. You need to know the financial health of your insurance company whenever you consider buying life insurance, because you are likely making a contract for 20, 30, or 50 years, and you want the company to keep their end of the bargain when that time comes. Ratings start at A++ for a truly superior company and go all the way to S, which means they're so far in the hole that we don't even rate them anymore. I recommend you don't buy anything long term from a company rated lower than B+. Here's the rating scale used by A. M. Best—the column labels are theirs too:

Secure	Vulnerable
A++, A+ (Superior)	B, B–(Fair)
A, A–(Excellent)	C++, C+ (Marginal)
B++, B+ (Good)	C, C–(Weak)
	D (Poor)
	E (Under regulatory supervision)
	F (In liquidation)
	S (Rating suspended)

Want to check out your insurer, actual or contemplated? Go to www.ambest.com. They'll require you to register—who doesn't these days—but there's no charge. You can opt out of getting future emails, and it's good for a long time.

If you've never shopped for life insurance before, this will hopefully help you make some decisions without the assistance of an insurance salesperson at your elbow.

Whole Life Insurance

This is the kind that lasts forever as long as you pay the premium. You have a fixed amount of insurance (that may grow with certain options but will never shrink) for your lifetime, and the premium is also fixed for as long as you own the policy. And because premiums include a mandatory savings feature, a portion of your premium goes to build an asset for you called *cash surrender value.* This is the amount that you can borrow at any time, as long as the premiums have been paid, and the company will pay you this amount in cash if you ever decide you don't want the policy anymore and are willing to surrender it. Thus, the name. Your policy is required to include a table that shows you the cash surrender value at any time during the life of your policy, year by year. If you borrow against this for any reason, any unpaid amounts are deducted from the proceeds of the policy in the event the insured person dies.

Why buy whole life insurance? Because the premium can never be raised no matter the state of your health.

Term Insurance

This is like whole life insurance stripped down to its bare minimum, with no savings features, no cash surrender value, and no borrowing capability. But the cost is a lot lower than whole life insurance. If you want just insurance, without the bells and whistles of whole life, and you want your insurance dollars to stretch, this is a good product to consider. I used it when I was raising a family and I wanted more pure protection than I could afford with whole life, and I wasn't going to need it forever.

This last part is important because of one other key difference compared to whole life policies. The premium goes up as you get older, and at some point it goes *way up*. As you keep living, it gets prohibitively expensive to keep the policy and continue paying the premium. In other words, you don't buy term insurance if you are thinking about leaving the proceeds to your children when you die of old age. You buy it early in life and look to replace it later on with more permanent insurance, such as whole life, or perhaps when you've made a fortune on your 401(k) and don't need insurance any longer. Just kidding.

Why buy term insurance? Because you need a lot of protection when your family is growing up and not so much when they're grown.

Mortgage Insurance

A variation of term insurance, this is a form of protection that is intended to protect you and your family from being without a home in the event the person earning the income to pay the mortgage loan dies. It's frequently a requirement of the mortgage lender if the borrower is unable to come up with a 20% down payment on the purchase. The idea is to protect the lender from being without a source of repayment and the family from being forced out of their home as a result of the death of the breadwinner.

A mortgage insurance policy starts with a certain amount of insurance, perhaps based on the difference between the borrower's actual down payment and the 20% down payment your mortgage lender would have preferred. Or you can buy insurance to cover the entire loan amount. Then as the loan balance gets paid down, the amount of insurance that the policy provides goes down too, automatically. This is called *decreasing term insurance* because the amount of coverage actually decreases over time. The downside of this insurance is that the homeowner has to pay the premium, but the mortgage lender is the beneficiary on the policy. They get the money, the survivors get the house. The good news: When the equity in the home reaches 20%, and assuming you no longer want to keep it, you can ask to have the mortgage insurance requirement removed, and the insurer is required to agree. There are ways to get this requirement waived, such as paying a larger interest rate on the loan, but that discussion is beyond the scope of this book. If you need to know more about this, you might check out the information available free at www.frbsf.org/publications/consumer, the information site of the Federal Reserve Bank of San Francisco.

Why buy mortgage insurance? Because you want your family to be able to keep your house, mortgage free, if you should die before it's paid off (or because the lender insisted on it).

Health Insurance: Staying Healthy

This is a huge area with seemingly endless options, and if you've held a job anywhere where the company provides benefits, including your school district, you probably know all this already. So forgive a few helpful hints for those who may be facing their first real job out of college, because they may not know this stuff yet.

Health insurance comes in various flavors and sizes, covering doctor visits, hospital stays, preventive and emergency care, and countless other ways you might need help in paying for your health care needs. Insurance programs are often tailored to fit the employer's budget, including or excluding benefits to keep the premium cost manageable. Employers will often share a portion of the premium cost with you, sometimes they'll even pay all of it for you but not for your family, and sometimes they'll pay a fixed dollar amount that you can use to purchase whatever coverage you choose to have. The doctors, hospitals, and drugstores are called providers, and providers are usually going to charge you a small amount called a co-payment—at least it's small compared to what they'll bill the insurance companies—each time you use their services. If FSAs and HSAs are available to you, you might want to reread the sections on them in Chapter 3.

There are basically two kinds of health insurance policies offered today, HMOs and PPOs. Huh? Health maintenance organizations and preferred provider organizations. Most benefit programs provided by employers will offer both options, although sometimes with slightly different names attached. Here's a quick look at the main differences:

	HMOs	PPOs
Source of service providers	A large network of providers who have signed up to be a part of that HMO's network	A wider network of providers who accept patients at the (higher) PPO-approved rates
Freedom to use your own providers	Usually not	Yes, but usually at some additional cost compared to the network
Premium cost to the company and the employee	Least expensive health care option available, typically	More expensive, often substantially more, than HMOs
Reason to make this choice	Low cost; no preference as to your doctor or other providers	You want to pick the doctor, and he or she isn't in the network

Incidentally, the above does not include dental insurance, vision insurance, or term life insurance, all of which are often available separately at additional cost.

Why buy health insurance? Because if you don't, you probably can't afford to get sick at today's health care costs and because your family will absolutely need it at some point.

Disability Insurance: In Case Something Breaks

When your employer deducts payroll taxes from your paycheck, a small part of that goes to your state to pay for disability insurance, a benefit that the state will pay you for short-term injuries or illnesses that prevent you from working. The benefit isn't a lot, but the assumption is your disability will be pretty short term, and you'll be back to work soon earning full pay. You are entitled to that benefit automatically because the state provides it.

If you want protection against possible longer-term disabilities, including those that might last for years, you will need to consider private, long-term disability insurance, typically available from many of the same companies that sell life insurance. Long-term disability insurance will pay a portion of your regular earnings for a given period of time after a waiting period, during which short-term disability insurance is supposed to provide assistance. For example, a policy might begin paying you 50% of your normal earnings after you've been off for 90 days and continue paying until you are back to work, or 5 years, whichever comes sooner. The premium for that coverage will likely cost you several hundred dollars a month or more, depending, among other things, on what percentage of your regular pay you want to insure.

Do you need this? A September 2008 article in *SmartMoney* had this quote: "The reality is one third of all Americans between the ages 35 and 65 will become disabled for more than 90 days, according to the American Council of Life Insurers."[1] If the breadwinner in your family is a diabetic, for example, the higher likelihood of missing work might dictate the need for such coverage, while a normally healthy family without such problems might not need it. As for the life insurance industry quote, it may be right on the money, although I tend to think such statistics are based on yesterday's data, and healthier lifestyles today make it likely that we'll be creating new and better statistics by the time we become the statistics. I had such a policy for 25 years and never used it, so I stopped paying the premium perhaps 10 years ago and still wouldn't have used it even to this day. Have I been lucky? Will you be as lucky? That's a decision you'll have to make for yourself.

Why buy disability insurance? Because you never know if you'll be one of those statistics. Feel lucky?

Long-Term Care Insurance: For the Later Years

What are the chances you will spend a few years in a nursing home when you get older? What are the chances your spouse will need in-home nursing care to be able to remain at home in his or her later years as opposed to a nursing facility? These options are the kinds of services that are provided by long-term care insurance. A relatively new product, probably invented because of the aging baby boomer generation, this insurance recognizes that the high cost of nursing care today would easily wipe out the assets of most elderly people if they didn't get help. The alternative is being on government assistance for elderly health care, and access to such assistance requires, in most cases, that the family surrender all material assets to the state. Clearly, neither of these is a pleasant option, so long-term care insurance is intended to fill the gap—Social Security doesn't pay for this kind of service—and enable the family to preserve its assets and still give aging family members the care they need.

---

1. http://www.smartmoney.com/personal-finance/insurance/do-you-need-disability-insurance-17318/

The coverage is usually defined by how much you want the policy to pay for each day of nursing care you will need. Today's costs are estimated to range between $100 and $400 a day, which means monthly costs could run to $12,000 or more, even higher if there is a great need for medication or around-the-clock care. The U.S. Department of Health and Human Services reports on its website that the average cost in the U.S. for a private room in a nursing home in 2008 was $209 a day.[2] That's $76,000 a year *average!* Major cities are much more. My father spent two years in a nursing home in Johnstown, Pennsylvania, before he died, suffering from both Alzheimer's and Parkinson's disease. Since he didn't care much for insurance, his widow paid over $6,000 a month for his care and medicine during that entire period. Imagine what that would do to your savings if you had to write those checks for a year or two.

There are additional parameters I've discovered as my wife and I shopped for ourselves, including these:

- How long of a waiting period before benefits begin to be paid—90 days, 180 days, and so forth
- How many years benefits will be paid—5 years, 10 years, a lifetime, and so on
- How old you are when you apply
- How healthy you are when you apply—no risky conditions wanted by the insurers
- Whether you want only one spouse or two covered—quantity discounts available
- Whether the benefits for husband and wife will be shared between them—a way to hedge against not knowing which spouse might need it, potentially at lower cost than buying two policies

There's another wrinkle in this kind of insurance. Since it's relatively new, insurers have been discovering the past few years that they underpriced it—charged less than it cost them to provide benefits. So all policies issued today have the provision that rates could increase in the future, a big contingency for a policy that is already as expensive as whole life insurance.

The two questions for you to ask yourself are these: (1) Should you buy it? (2) When should you buy it? The first is about the likelihood of you or your spouse needing it sometime, and the second is

2. http://www.longtermcare.gov/LTC/Main_Site/Paying_LTC/Costs_Of_Care/Costs_Of_Care.aspx#What

about managing the premium cost. The longer you wait to buy it, the longer you don't have to pay that premium, but the larger it will be when you do.

My Recommendation: I think waiting until later in life for this one is the wiser move financially; but since we don't know when we'll have the need or what future premiums will be, there is an element of risk in waiting. Ultimately, you must collect the information for yourself and decide what makes sense for your family.

Why buy long-term care insurance? Because long-term care can often consume all a couple's lifetime savings if one of you lives an extended, but infirmity-plagued, life.

SUMMARY OF KEY IDEAS FOR CHAPTER 6

1. You need life insurance. How much and what kind depends on the size of your family and your personal balance sheet. (Refer to Chapter 3.)

2. All insurance companies are not created equal. Some are stronger than others, and some just charge more than others so they can get stronger. Shop around before you sign up.

3. What kind of life insurance you buy is as important as how much. Choose whole life, term, or mortgage for the right reasons based on your need for protection.

4. Insurance is financial protection from the costs of injury or illness that you can't afford to pay for out of your regular income. Unless you feel lucky, you'll need most of these products at some time in your life.

7

Savings Accounts for Your Cash

The Value of Saving Early:
The Power of Compound Interest

When you lend your money to a bank, they will pay you interest for the privilege of using your money. Sometimes they pay a lot, sometimes not as much. When this book was written, the typical interest rate banks were paying for regular savings accounts was averaging 1% to 2%, not much to write home about. The best rates you could get for cash given to your local bank in early 2009 were still under 3%, and that was for a sizeable balance that you promised to let the bank keep for a year. Hard to make money at that rate, especially with any inflation at all.

Or is it? The inflation rate in early 2009 was virtually nonexistent. The federal Bureau of Labor Statistics, which tracks such things, reported that the actual inflation rate was less than zero during the summer,[1] meaning that prices were actually going down. During much of the decade of the 1990s, average interest rates for those big balances committed for a year were around 5%, and the inflation rate ranged from 2% to 3% a year. If you'll notice those comparisons, the difference or spread between the savings rate and the rate at which prices were going up, in both cases, is about 2% to 3 %. We'll call that the real savings rate, meaning the amount by which you actually get ahead, before taxes.

---

1. http://www.inflationdata.com/inflation/Inflation_Rate/HistoricalInflation.aspx

What if that were the best it could be? What if a real savings rate of 3% was the limit? It isn't, by the way, as you'll learn later in this book, but just pretend, as the kids say. What could that be worth?

First, I'll introduce some terminology—but just one term: *compounding*. Compounding is what happens when your interest earns interest, thus helping your savings to grow faster. Daily compounding means that each day the amount of your savings balance that earns interest is the sum of the amount you had in the account the day before plus the interest earned that day. In other words, the interest amount earns interest immediately after it gets into your account. Banks typically compound either daily or monthly, but the difference is relatively small. It's the compounding that matters, as you'll see below.

OK, here's an example with two scenarios.

First scenario: You invest $100 a month at 3% interest, net of inflation, for 20 years. The interest compounds daily. You let the money accumulate untouched for the entire 20 years as a college fund for those kids you haven't had yet. What would you have at the end?

- Without interest at all (you put it under the mattress), you'd have $100 × 12 months × 20 years, or $24,000. That will just about pay for 1.5 years of tuition, room, and board at a 4-year *public* university.[2] No books, though.
- With interest at 3% simple interest, no compounding, you'd have $24,000 plus interest for 20 years, or $31,131. That will pay for tuition and room and board for a year at a 4-year *private* university.[3] Still no books, though.
- With interest at 3% compounded daily, you'd have $32,764, an extra $1,600 to cover books, some social life, and perhaps some new sneakers as well.

Now, second scenario: You tap a hidden war chest and put the entire $24,000 in the bank on Day 1 and leave it there for 20 years with no monthly additions. It's the same total investment at the same 3% interest.

- Left in the mattress, of course, you'd still have only $24,000 of very wrinkled money.
- With no compounding of interest, you'd have $38,203 in the bank when junior heads to school, because more of your money had more time to earn interest. Now your child's even got a car to drive home in.

---

2. http://nces.ed.gov/fastfacts/display.asp?id=76

3. http://nces.ed.gov/fastfacts/display.asp?id=76

- With compounding, you'd now have $43,341, a college fund fattened by over $5,000 because it had the opportunity to let compound interest do its magic. Unless college costs go crazy, this money is *yours!*

We get two lessons from this little example—one obvious and one not so obvious. Money accumulates faster if you invest it sooner rather than later, and money accumulates faster with compound interest than with simple interest. When saving for any goal, both principles are good to keep in mind.

How Much Cash Can You Save?

If you're in the early years of your teaching career, you probably think it's pretty near impossible to live nicely on less than you take home each month. People who come around talking about savings accounts are shown the door pretty quickly because they just don't know what it takes to live on a teacher's salary, or they wouldn't be expecting you to live on even less than that. And you'd be right.

And we still have to talk about it.

My hope is that after reading six chapters, I've got you hooked enough on my thought process that you'll at least read what I have to say on the subject. Better yet, you're convinced even without a motivational talk that somehow you've got to squeeze out enough cash to be prepared for the things that come up in everyday life that you couldn't anticipate or pay for as they come up.

When it comes to safety, there's nothing quite like cash, especially if you put it into a bank in increments of $100,000 or less. Every cash account from $1 to $100,000 that is placed with a registered bank overseen by the U.S. government is guaranteed by Uncle Sam to be paid to you without hesitation even if that bank goes out of business. This is a very powerful protection, and it is why so many financial institutions that weren't banks converted to become banks in the 2008–2009 credit meltdown, so they could have their customer balances covered by that insurance policy. The federal government even raised the maximum amount they would ensure to $250,000 for a while to help people overcome the fear of their banks failing.

Saving money is an interesting example of compounding. If you save $5 a day for an emergency that doesn't happen, and that is your daily pattern, tomorrow you'll have $10, and in a year you'll have about $1,875 at 5% interest, or some number resembling that. In 20 years that $5-a-day plan will have produced $62,500, give or take a little income tax. Of course that assumes you never need the money, and the whole point is to have it available if you do need it. So how much should you have in the mattress, the savings account (same thing these days), or some other readily available stash? Let's see.

The Rainy-Day Fund

Lots of financial advisers will tell you it's wise planning to have about 6 months of expenses in your rainy-day fund. That's a hefty chunk of change for most of us, and it's not any easier if you have a modest salary, a growing family, and a thirst to experience a new side of life over summer vacation. I agree with them in principle, but let's take a closer look at that idea, because the numbers may not be as big as you think. Consider Table 7.1, showing the kinds of expenses that are typical for an average household. The amounts are made up and may look unrealistic to you based on your lifestyle, but the concept is real at any income level.

With no representation that this is a complete list, or that it's even your list, there is a point to be made here: As your career progresses, as your life progresses, your spending patterns will change. And when life events occur that impact your income, like summer unemployment or retirement, you will be able to find lots of ways to reduce your spending, probably dramatically. And that's the point. You don't need to save emergency funds at the rate you currently spend; you need to save emergency funds at the rate you would spend if you were in that emergency.

I know that you may very well want to spend money on things that I've not listed, and of course that's fine. But for now, we're focusing on what you *have to* spend, not the options that you choose to add to the list because you're not ready to give them up. If your income enables you to keep expenses such as travel and gifts for special occasions, that's great. But do you need to have a rainy-day fund for those things? Maybe not.

So if you think about the things you wouldn't spend money on if you were faced with a financial emergency, and the things you could postpone spending money on until the emergency passed, your savings nut isn't as big as it sounds. Still it's money most would rather have available to spend today, and that's understandable. At the risk of repeating myself, *there's always a good reason to spend money, but that doesn't always mean it's a good idea.*

But it's always a good idea to start building a rainy-day fund before you tackle any of the strategies that occupy the rest of this book.

Table 7.1	Typical Monthly Living Expenses at Different Stages of Life			
	Typical Expense Early Career	Typical Expense Late Career	Typical Expense if Out of Work	Typical Expense if Permanently Retired
Bank charges	10	10	10	10
Car expenses	100	100	50	50
Clothing	200	150	0	25
Contributions	25	50	0	15
Dining out	100	150	0	50
Dues and subscriptions	15	15	0	0
Career development	100	50	0	0
Entertainment	100	150	0	25
Gifts	25	50	0	20
Groceries	250	350	175	175
Household repairs	75	75	0	25
TV service	60	75	25	50
Insurance, auto	75	50	50	50
Insurance, home	100	125	100	125
Insurance, health	200	300	200	75
Insurance, life	50	50	50	50
Medical care	200	300	100	50
Rent/Mortgage	1,000	2,000	1,000	0
Personal services	50	75	25	25
School materials	25	50	0	0
Taxes, income	500	750	0	200
Tax preparation fees	40	50	50	50
Telephone	100	150	75	75
Travel	400	800	0	800
Utilities	150	200	150	150
Total	3,950	6,125	2,060	2,095

Savings Accounts

The simplest form of savings is a good, old-fashioned, bank-provided savings account. You put in money, and they lend it to someone and pay you a portion of what they earn. At least that's the bank's plan. When things go wrong for them, as they have the past couple years, banks will pay you as little as possible on your savings account to make up for other things they've done that have gone south on them. Today, many savings accounts pay less than 1% annually, and most pay less than 2%, which means that with any inflation at all, you're not actually saving money. Rather, it's just depleting more slowly. My personal view is that you should use a savings account to accumulate that 5-dollars-a-day money, and keep it there only until you have accumulated enough to put it somewhere else. Plus, of course, it's a good way to teach your young children a savings habit until they have saved enough to put it somewhere else. I have a savings account that gets money for a near-term purchase that I want to pay cash for or for taxes that come due at known intervals during the year. That's it. So let's move on with our cash to the next step up.

Money Market Funds

These are actually a form of mutual fund—which I'll talk about much more in Chapter 10—or pools of dollars that some professional money manager uses to make very safe investments that will earn more than you could earn with your savings account. The fund manager will buy U.S. Treasury bonds, for example, which are what the government gives you when it borrows your money to finance the federal deficit. They are in effect lending your money to the government. Those bonds pay more than savings accounts, and they're 100% guaranteed by, you guessed it, the U.S. government. That will typically be the core of most money market funds, so that they can easily pay off any requests to cash out from folks like us.

But please note: While some of the money market fund's investments are insured by the U.S. government, the money market fund itself, and the shares you purchase in the fund, are *not* insured.

Then these same money managers will attempt to improve their returns—for their benefit and yours—by adding to their portfolio some higher-earning debt from presumably excellent sources, but not so excellent as Uncle Sam. These bonds and similar investments will pay more interest and have more risk attached to them, but by managing the mix, the professionals hope to raise the yield without getting caught with any defaults. Typical examples might be high-grade bonds of large corporations with excellent credit ratings or perhaps some debt backed by solid mortgage loans that are, in turn, backed by real estate. Money market funds typically pay more interest than insured deposits because they are taking more risk and therefore will earn a higher return if everything goes well.

It will take you only a moment to realize that this last item has probably caused some funds a hiccup or two in the past year or so as the credit crunch and housing collapse caused a lot of mortgage loans to go unpaid, surprising lots of investors, as it turned out. It's a good idea to inquire about the kind of instruments your money market fund might be investing in before you purchase because, remember, money market funds are not insured by the government. Rarely will there be a problem getting your money back, but 2008 was one of those rare occasions. So play it safe by asking, but think of money market funds as a good place to put your short-term cash to work.

Certificates of Deposit

At the top of the cash stash option list, in terms of return, is the certificate of deposit (CD) that your bank will give you if you are willing to commit to leaving your money with them for a fixed period of time. That fixed period of time may be as little as a month or as much as several years, and the rate of interest they will pay will vary based on the amount you have to deposit and the length of your commitment. Typically, that means the more money you commit and the longer you commit it for, the higher the rate you will earn, because the bank doesn't have to worry about having the money around to pay you back. But it's not as simple as that, wouldn't you know. Banks compete against one another for your deposits most of the time, so rates will differ from bank to bank depending on how badly one bank wants your money compared to their competitors on any given day. To take this a step further, banks will establish internal profiles that they want to maintain—so much in deposits that is locked up for 6 months, so much for a year, so much for 2 years, and so forth. Bank A's success in getting all the 2-year deposits it wants is likely to cause them to lower the rate they will pay for more 2-year money. As a result, there may be a sizeable difference between Bank A's rate for 2-year CDs and Bank B's across the street, with the same government protections for the same 2-year CD. The moral of the story: Shop around. Rates in mid-2009 were still not great, ranging from 3% to 4%, but that's double the typical savings account rate.

SUMMARY OF KEY IDEAS FOR CHAPTER 7

1. Compound interest is your reward for lending your money to a bank and letting it accumulate untouched. If you lend them a lot of money for a long time, you'll be amazed at how much it will grow.

2. Saving money for a rainy day, or unemployment, can sound overwhelming if you look at what you spend today. But if you look at how your expenses could decline if necessary, it becomes a lot more feasible to build that rainy-day fund without actually causing rain.

3. Your savings should come before you start an investment program. Where you put your savings—bank account, money market fund, certificates of deposit—depends on your desire for higher returns, your willingness to commit your cash for a period of time, and your tolerance for a little risk.

8

Buying a Home

Realizing the American Dream

I f you're reading this book, it's safe to say you are among the major-
ity of Americans who believe that owning their own home is an
important family financial goal. Home ownership has been the cornerstone of personal wealth in America since its founding, I imagine,
and certainly for as long as I've been old enough to read. For most of
us, our home is the largest asset we will ever buy, and the most valuable, although it may not necessarily be the best investment in the
future. Many of us will buy several of these over our lifetimes, but
rarely more than one at a time. Why? Because they cost a lot of money,
mostly. The average public schoolteacher's salary, according to a
2006–2007 survey by the American Federation of Teachers (AFT), was
$51,009[1] a year (less for charter schools). Allowing for a 4% annual
increase would get it to about $55,200 in 2009. The average home in
America was estimated to have a value of $251,000 in April 2009,
according to the U.S. Census Bureau.[2] The trick is making the first
number large enough to pay for the second one while feeding and

---

1. 2007 Survey and Analysis of Teacher Salary Trends—The average salary for traditional
public school teachers increased 4.5% in 2006–2007 to $51,009, according to the AFT's
latest teacher salary survey, marking the first time average teacher pay exceeded
$50,000 and the first time since 2003 that teacher salaries surpassed the annual rate of
inflation. The AFT report also includes never-before-released salary data for charter
schoolteachers in 29 states—of the 40 that have charter schools—where the news was
not as positive. The average charter schoolteacher salary was $41,106, nearly $10,000
less than that for traditional public schoolteachers.

2. http://www.census.gov/const/uspricemon.pdf

clothing its occupants as well. So what should you know before you set out to fulfill that particular life goal?

Well, first of all, it would be good to forget the experience of home price appreciation during the past 10 years or so, because most experts tell us it didn't used to be like that and it is unlikely to be like that again anytime soon, if ever. So don't count on building a large amount of wealth through home ownership. Rather, count on being able to provide a secure, comfortable home for your family to grow up in. If you can make some money when you sell, all the better.

How Much Home Can You Afford?

Well, the answer to this key question very much depends on whom you ask. In *The Complete Idiot's Guide to Buying and Selling a Home*, Shelley O'Hara and Nancy D. Warner estimate that a buyer should plan to borrow "roughly 2 to 2½ times your annual gross salary. If you and your partner together make $50,000, for example, you might be able to buy a home in the $100,000 to $125,000 range."[3] The authors advise against a strict interpretation of this ballpark method, since all couples earning $50,000 aren't equal. One may have $50,000 in savings and no car payment, which should qualify them for an even higher loan. Another couple, however, might have two car payments, maxed-out credit cards, and no down payment, which won't qualify them for a home in any price range.

When I tested the average teacher's salary against a calculator on the GNMA site (Government National Mortgage Association,[4] the government-owned corporation that guarantees home mortgages), it told me a teacher with the average salary, a spouse, two children, and $1,000 in monthly living expenses could afford a home costing $102,000, but only if they put up a $15,000 down payment (monthly payment $520). In most places, that wouldn't get you very much room for four people. But when I put the same information into a calculator at www.bankrate.com, I was told that the same teacher could afford a $229,000 home (monthly payment $1,100), almost the U.S. average. I think Bankrate.com assumed you wouldn't have to feed the kids every day, which could save quite a bit of money. Or maybe they just assumed the reality of home ownership today—maybe they also counted your spouse's income as well as yours in order to afford much more than a starter home. Two teachers each making $55,000,

---

3. http://www.salary.com/personal/layoutscripts/psnl_articles.asp?tab=psn&cat=cat011&ser=ser035&part=par236

4. http://www.ginniemae.gov/2_prequal/intro_questions.asp?section=YPTH

for example, could afford a $201,000 home using an FHA (Federal Housing Administration) mortgage, according to GNMA.

So what's the real answer? There really isn't one. It depends on you. This is where your work in Chapter 2 becomes important. If you have a family budget, you will know how much discretionary income you have and how much of that you are willing to invest in a long-term commitment like a mortgage loan. If there's one thing the home price crash of 2008 told us, it's that buying more house than you can afford to pay for is a recipe for financial failure that could weigh you down for years to come.

Still, by the time you read this, there may still be some awesome bargains in home prices as banks and mortgage holders unload the balance of their inventory of foreclosed homes. During 2008 and 2009, a record number of foreclosures sank market prices, creating misery for some and buying opportunities for others. If that's still the situation where you live, you may very well be able to buy a very nice home for $100,000 or so in some parts of the country. My sister bought a brand-new, never-been-lived-in, three-bedroom home near Tampa, Florida, for about $120,000 in early 2009, an unheard-of bargain only months earlier.

Chapter 14 talks about using a financial planner to help you in retirement planning, but you might want to consider getting some of that help when it's time to buy your first home as well. The cost is much less than the cost of a foreclosure. And the joy and sense of security that come from owning your own home—well, it's worth the effort to do it right the first time.

If you have not yet purchased any real estate, the information that follows will hopefully help you make payment decisions when the time comes. Depending on the kind of loan you have obtained, your payment will include, as a minimum, principal and interest. At first, the principal (the portion of your payment that actually reduces your loan balance) will be very small—I mean *very* small—and you'll wonder how the loan will ever get paid off at that rate. But keep in mind that the payment was probably calculated on the assumption that you would make that payment for 30 years, or 360 payments. Like water on a rock, that kind of steady flow can wear down even the sturdiest of loans. It takes only a $665 payment at a 7% interest rate to pay off a $100,000 loan in 30 years.

To calculate your payment on any mortgage, an automatic mortgage calculator is a very handy tool to have on your computer. The best one I've found is at www.rentalsoftware.com, and you can use it by purchasing the product directly or downloading a version of it at www.corwin.com/financialmastery, along with my other spreadsheet templates.

So let's get some of the arcane financial language of home ownership out of the way.

First Mortgage, Second Mortgage, Equity Credit Lines: The Language of Real Estate Finance

These are all tools you will use to finance the portion of the home that you won't pay for in cash, which is probably most of it. Virtually every home purchase comes with a *mortgage* or *trust deed*, which is a lien on your property that the lender will keep until you pay off the loan. That mortgage is the document you will sign that gives the bank the right to repossess the house if you don't make your payments. It will be accompanied by another document, a note payable to the bank that outlines the payment terms, interest rate, and the amount of your monthly payment. You are actually making payments on the note, not the mortgage, but we tend to interchange the two in conversation, so don't worry too much about that. Also, terms of your mortgage may differ widely from state to state, so you'll want to read the fine print carefully and have someone explain anything you don't understand. Do yourself a favor, and don't rely on the bank or the mortgage broker to do all the explaining.

When you buy a home, the amount financed is secured by the mortgage. Your monthly payment is composed of a month's interest on the loan balance and a (smaller) amount that reduces the loan balance (the *principal payment*). The payment of principal is called *amortization* in real estate talk, meaning the loan balance is being amortized or gradually reduced. So your monthly payment includes both principal and interest as a minimum. As you make payments, you reduce the loan balance and increase your share of ownership in your home as a result. That's called *equity*. Equity is measured at any given time by the difference between the current market value of your home (*not* what you paid for it) and the amount you still owe on the loan. As the value of your home increases, that too creates equity, at least on paper. Equity comes from three sources:

- The amount of your down payment
- The principal portion of your loan payments
- The increase in value of your home if prices are appreciating

As many have learned recently, that last item can go either way. A decrease in the value of your home will reduce your equity, potentially to the point that it can wipe out all the equity built up by the first two items on the list. However, over time, assuming your home appreciates in value and you have made your payments faithfully, you may have another borrowing option. If your equity becomes large enough, you will be able to obtain an additional loan without paying off your first one. For example, you may need to raise some money for a major home repair or other needs. If that happens, you may be able to get a bank to make a loan based on the equity in your home.

That second loan on your home equity will be secured by a *second mortgage,* and your original mortgage now becomes the *first mortgage.* You will now have two loans and two liens on your home, a first mortgage and a second mortgage, often from two different banks, to which you will make two separate, monthly payments. While first mortgages are typically set to be repaid in 30 years, second mortgages are often due in a much shorter time, perhaps 10 to 15 years. Also, the interest rate on the second mortgage will typically be 2% to 4% higher than the first mortgage, because that new loan has a secondary claim on your home (the *collateral*) in the event you don't make your payments, so it is a higher-risk loan for the bank.

Balloon Payments: A Funny Name for a Not-So-Funny Event

Let's suppose you go shopping for a second mortgage loan to finance your kids' education fund. The bank agrees to lend you the money and says something cryptic like, "Thirty-year amortization, due in 10." No problem, you got the loan, right? Not so fast. Let's make sure we know what that means. You will make payments on that loan that are small and manageable, perhaps $80 or so for each $10,000 you borrowed—but for only 10 years. At the end of that time, you're going to get a notice from the bank that the remaining 20 years of payments are due in 30 days! Ouch! So even if the payments on that loan are calculated on a 30-year payoff, they will often come with a *due in full* provision after 10 or 15 years. The balance that would be due at that time is called a *balloon payment,* and it almost always means you will need to refinance that mortgage in order to avoid paying off the balloon all at one time (unless you have made extra principal payments along the way). This is how banks and other lenders protect themselves from rapidly rising interest rates—they get the money repaid or refinanced at then-current interest rates instead of waiting another 20 years to get their money back. If interest rates are lower at the due date, you win. You get to refinance at a lower interest rate, thus your payments will be lower. If rates are higher when it's time to refinance, the bank wins. They get to lend you the same amount of money and get paid more each month in interest. Sometimes bank lending rates are based in part on their estimate of what rates will look like when it's time to renew, even though that is generally an educated guess at best.

The Home Equity Line of Credit

Now let's suppose you want the ability to borrow against that equity, but you don't want to borrow the whole thing all at once. You don't have an immediate need, but you want to make it possible to raise money quickly if that need should arise. That is the purpose of a *home equity line of credit*, or HELOC in bank speak. When you get a HELOC, you apply for a loan secured by a second mortgage, just as in the discussion above. But instead of getting a check from the bank for your loan amount, you get a checkbook. You will then decide when you want to borrow against that HELOC by simply writing a check, which you either deposit into your checking account or pay someone with. That action triggers a loan on the bank's books when they honor the check you've written for the exact amount of your check. From then on, interest charges begin accruing until that loan has been repaid. Payment terms will vary, but you will have a monthly payment to make based on the amount you borrowed, just as in the one-time loans above. As long as you have any unused credit availability on the HELOC, you can continue to write checks and add to the loan balance as needed.

Lines of credit are a great convenience because of the check-writing feature and the ability to pay back your HELOC loans at any time and then reborrow as often as needed. However, it would seem that with every advantage comes a disadvantage. The disadvantage in this case is the same as the advantage. It's easy to borrow, and people sometimes forget they are borrowing against their homes. Using that money for casual expenses, such as a dream vacation or a lifestyle in which expenses exceed income, can result in depleting the most valuable asset you own without getting any lasting value in return. And if that weren't enough of a disadvantage, these loans are usually variable-rate loans, so rates can change over time, and finally, the bank can choose to withdraw access to the unused portion of the line at any time, as many homeowners learned recently.

Structuring Your Payments:
Taxes, Insurance, and Impounds

So we've covered principal and interest. That takes care of the loan itself. Now what about your property taxes and property insurance? Property taxes, according to www.moneycentral.msn.com, currently range anywhere from .17% of the purchase price annually (Louisiana) to 1.82% (Texas and Wisconsin).[5] You will get a property tax bill every year, typically payable in two installments a few months apart. Nonpayment of property taxes can result in the taxing authorities becoming the new owners of your home, so you want to include those in your budget.

The cost of your insurance, providing protection from fire, flood, and lawsuits from someone who trips on your steps, will depend on the kind of coverage you purchased as well as the home price and will usually be due annually unless you can arrange a monthly or quarterly plan with your insurer. Be aware that the monthly and quarterly plans have fees added that amount to a pretty hefty interest rate for the amount of money you're borrowing just to pay for insurance in installments. It's best to pay them a year at a time if you can. Want a better option? Read on.

You can pay those annual costs when the bill arrives from the tax collector and your insurance company, and from a purely financial standpoint, that is the smart thing to do. But I've always found those bills to be something of a shock when they arrive. So I've always preferred to pay them monthly rather than all at once, even if I have to pay up front before the bills actually arrive. The way to do that without the interest charges or risk of tax liens mentioned above is to arrange an *impound account* with the mortgage lender. They bill you for a portion of the taxes and insurance each month (or just one or the other, at your option), and they make your payments for you without any further action on your part. This involves giving your lender some of your money to keep all year long, typically interest free (unless your state requires that balances earn interest), in return for not having to handle those big bills when they're due. Alternatively, if you are a steady saver, the smart move is to put the equivalent amount into a savings account each month so you'll have the money to make those taxes and insurance payments, and you'll earn a little interest. Most of us are not good at the saving part, unfortunately, which is why I usually suggest you just go with the impound account. The interest income you forgo is nothing to write home about, and the peace of mind is nice.

One final thought on impounds: I've written about them as an option you can choose. But if you have made less than a 20% down payment on your home, it is likely that your lender will require an impound account as a condition of the loan to ensure that the property

5. http://www.articles.moneycentral.msn.com, February 7, 2007, "Property taxes: Where does your state rank?"

stays free of liens and is protected from physical loss. Such a requirement can be removed once your equity grows to 20%.

Refinancing for Cash-Out, for Lower Rates, for Better Terms

One of the interesting phenomena of the past few years of widely fluctuating interest rates has been the opportunity to refinance your home loan to get better interest rates or terms or even to get cash by borrowing some of the equity you've built up. When you refinance, you are finding a lender to pay off your current mortgage loan (and your second mortgage loan, if you have one) and give you a new loan. Some of the reasons you might want to do that include the following:

- A loan that you can pay off in 15 years instead of 30 years, thus being payment-free sooner
- A loan with a fixed interest rate instead of a variable one
- A conversion of equity into cash to pay off bills that carry higher interest rates or larger payments or just to get some cash to spend elsewhere
- A loan with a lower interest rate than you have now
- A balloon payment that has come due

As the government has used interest rates more aggressively as a tool to manage the economy, the opportunities for big changes in interest rates have become more frequent, and I suspect most homeowners in the United States have refinanced their loans at least once in the past few years. I refinanced mine three times over a 7-year period, each time for a lower interest rate.

Variable Interest Rate Loans: A Good Deal or Not? Yes and No

In the past 10 or 15 years, a phenomenon has arisen that didn't exist when our parents bought their first home—the variable interest rate loan, often referred to in real estate speak as ARMs (adjustable rate mortgages). When you have such a loan, your interest rate will change if interest rates in the market go up or down during the term of your loan. When that happens, your loan payment will increase or decrease so that the loan will still be fully paid off in the time provided for in the loan documents—for example, 30 years. Some of these loans provide for a fixed rate for a few years—often referred to as *teaser rates*—and then an automatic conversion to a variable rate for the balance of the loan. You have likely read a lot about this in the past couple years, as ARMs were freely granted to home buyers who were not prepared for the upward adjustments of interest rates and monthly payments.

But shenanigans aside, an ARM can be a good idea if you plan to stay in this home for only a few years. The fixed rate converting to variable rate might work because the fixed rate is typically very low, and you would expect to sell the home before the fixed-rate period ends. Or the variable rate might be low enough that even if it works its way up, you have still saved money by the time you sell. Or the interest rate climate might be such that rates are on a long-term decline or are stable, in which case, the rate would have no reason to adjust upward (the challenge here is that none of us has a good enough crystal ball to know the future course of interest rates).

Getting Cash-Out Through Refinancing: The Good, the Bad, and the Really Bad

When home prices climb, as they did through much of the past decade, people have a lot of equity in their homes, and it's easy to see equity as money sitting there not doing anything for you, especially if paying the bills is getting more difficult. Many homeowners took advantage of the easy refinancing terms to get new loans for larger amounts of money than they originally borrowed so they could get a fresh start by paying off expensive credit card bills, put a pool in the backyard, take a dream vacation, or free up money to invest elsewhere. All that can be good. Home loan rates are almost always less than credit card rates, and a dollar of interest not paid is a dollar saved. And opportunities to improve your home, take a memorable vacation, or make a good investment all sound like potentially positive ways to use your equity. But it's good to keep in mind that you are spending your wealth when you do this, so it's not to be taken lightly, which gets me to the bad part.

Paying off the credit cards without a sense of discipline to keep credit card balances from growing again is a recipe for disaster—depleting your wealth over time without realizing it. It masks the fact that you may be living beyond your means by spending more than you earn, and that has caused many a cardholder to go from homeowner to bankruptcy court. And while credit cards are the easiest way to overspend, any lifestyle that does not provide for reasonable savings is heading in the same direction. The financial management tools spoken of elsewhere in this book are the best way to avoid this really bad possibility.

Getting a Lower Interest Rate on
Your Loan: The Real Deal if You Do It Right

In my opinion, this is the only reason to refinance that has almost no downside. And if you can get a no-points-and-no-fees loan, it has no downside at all. Refinancing a 9% loan and replacing it with a 7% loan is a wonderful thing to behold, and it will put a sizeable chunk of cash in your pocket every month if you do it right. The main thing to be wary of is the cost of refinancing. During periods of high competition among lenders, you can find a broker who will refinance your loan and not charge you any *points*[6] or fees because the lending bank is willing to pay the broker fees and refinance costs to get your loan business. At other times, most of those fees can be built into the loan balance—you owe a bit more but don't have to write a big check to get the refinancing done. However, refinancing a 9% loan for an 8.5% loan and paying two points in fees to do it is a bad idea. You are paying more than you're getting in value, and your home could easily cost you more than if you had stayed with the higher-rate loan.

So how do you determine when the rate differential is good enough? Here's a quick way to estimate that. You'll need a calculator for this one, or you can use the online calculator at www.corwin.com/financialmastery.

Annual interest rate (rate on the note, not the annual percentage rate, APR, which includes fees and add-ons) you now pay	8.5% or .085
Annual interest rate with a refinance (again, not the APR)	7.3% or .073
The difference per year	1.2% or .012
The difference per month (annual rate difference divided by 12)	.1% or .001
Monthly cash savings on a $100,000 loan = $100,000 × .001	$100
Total fees you must pay or add to your loan to get this done	$5,000
Number of months it will take you to break even ($5,000/$100)	50

That's how long it will take for you to recover the fees and begin actually saving money on the refinance, ignoring any interest on the amount saved over time. If that length of time is significantly less than the time you plan to be in the home, it's probably a good idea. If there are no fees, it's a good idea from day one. If neither of these is the case, the refinance could cost you more in the long run than you

---

6. A point is 1% of the total amount of the loan.

will save, and you may want to ask yourself why you would want to do this.

Teaser Rates, Interest Only, Negative Amortization, and Other Financial Land Mines

There are some variations of the loan types mentioned above that require special mention because, like a strong drug, they appeal to the senses while sapping the life out of your finances. I recommend you avoid these totally, unless you consider yourself a strong and dispassionate financial manager (in which case I doubt if you'd be reading my book).

Teaser Rates. Many of the foreclosures and trustee sales of the recent housing crisis were precipitated by the availability of teaser rates, unrealistically low rates for a short period of time that then moved up to market rates with an accompanying big boost in the monthly payment. Families moved into homes with payments that they could easily afford without sufficient thought to what they would do after the teaser rates were adjusted. Some rates were as low as 1% or 2% annually, but for 6 months or 9 months or a year only. With very little equity to fight for, when they found they couldn't handle the adjusted payment, they just moved out or lived there until the authorities evicted them months later, destroying whatever credit rating they had in the process. My advice: In any financing negotiation, make your decision based on the rate *after* the teaser rate, not on the teaser rate itself.

Interest-Only Loans. Closely related to teaser rates are interest-only loans in which no payment is required on principal for some period of time, from a few months to a few years, during which time the loan balance never goes down, and homeowners never build a single dollar of equity beyond their original down payment and any appreciation in home prices. These loans can be a good idea for people with a highly volatile flow of income—for example, salespeople, as long as they pay down principal when times are good so they can be more frugal and pay interest only when times are not so good. The problem is that people get used to the interest-only payment, obviously smaller than a payment that includes principal. When the interest-only period ends—as it must—they are not prepared to ratchet up their payment to the new amount, which is by then larger than it originally would have been if they'd been paying down principal all along. It's potentially useful, but not for the faint of heart.

Negative Amortization Loans. This is the land mine that truly destroys. Not a teaser-rate loan that pays down only the smallest principal and then goes up a few months later, not a loan that prevents the loan balance from ever going down; this is a loan that actually has the loan balance go *up!* Offered during the most aggressive marketing periods for lenders, these loans have payments so small for some period of time that they don't even pay the interest on the loan. And when your loan payment isn't large enough to cover the interest, what do you suppose the lender does with the difference? They add it to your loan balance so that the next month you owe more, and your interest is also more because it's based on the loan balance. A variation of this idea is the option ARM, or flexible payment ARM, in which borrowers can choose the payment they want to make each month: a fully amortizing payment, an interest-only payment, or a smaller payment that involves negative amortization. Again, this is one more method of giving people who could not afford to buy a home the opportunity to buy one anyway. Many of these borrowers never made a fully amortized payment, because they couldn't.

Final Thoughts on Mortgage Loans. If you're getting the impression that I don't recommend negative amortization or Option ARM loans, you'd be right. I suggest that only under very special circumstances should you consider anything but a fixed-rate, 30-year mortgage. What are those very special circumstances? Only two, really. You might consider a *reverse mortgage* in your retirement planning—not discussed here; read about them in Chapter 14. Or you might consider a straight variable interest loan (ARM) in the following situations:

1. The rate differential compared to a fixed-rate loan is large, meaning you are saving a lot of interest every month.

2. You have determined that the interest you save cannot be recouped by the lender during the period of time you will own that home, even if rates go up the maximum they can under your loan's rate change provisions. If this is not a calculation you know how to make, and your lender or mortgage broker can't or won't make it for you, email me at gene@genesiciliano .com, and I'll walk you through it (assuming you are the owner of this book, of course).

Final Thoughts on Home Ownership

You should, in my opinion, plan to own your home at some point in your career and from then on until you retire. Home ownership is not always the best purely financial investment you will make, but it brings with it a whole lot of comfort in the knowledge that you have control over where you live and how you live, and you are building equity in the process. That twofold benefit is worth more than money, and the fact that you are accumulating wealth in the process, albeit not at breakneck speed, makes it a must-have in your financial planning. Just my opinion.

The American dream is alive and well in America.

SUMMARY OF KEY IDEAS FOR CHAPTER 8

1. Don't look for a magic formula that translates your salary into the price of a home you should buy. There isn't one that really works without your also looking at your savings and monthly expenses.

2. The fine print in every real estate loan seems to discourage any attempt to actually read it. Do it anyway, because the fine print often contains unpleasant surprises that you need to know about *before* you sign.

3. Refinancing your loan to get a lower interest rate is usually a good idea, but make sure the loan fees don't eat up all the savings you thought you were getting. Calculate how long it will take to recoup those fees before saying yes.

4. Before you accept any loan other than a 30-year, fixed-rate repayment plan, ask yourself why you are doing this, and be sure that the answer makes financial sense, as opposed to being the means to get into a larger home than you could otherwise afford.

5. Do not, under any circumstances, accept a negative amortization loan. If this is what it takes to buy the home you are considering, the house is too expensive for you, and that will come back to haunt you in the future.

9

The Stock Market

All About Bulls and Bears

I firmly believe some portion of everyone's investment portfolio should be in the stock market in some form. It is, in my opinion, the best way to participate in the capitalist economic system that made this country great.

The market is a very big topic to cover in a single chapter, so I've broken it into two chapters. There are so many ways to approach investing in securities (the generic label for stocks, bonds, mutual funds, etc.) that the most we can do here is to help you get familiar with the more common terms, the types of investment strategies, and some of the caveats of investing. We'll cover the kinds of securities, types of investment approaches, and long-term versus short-term investing, and we'll end the chapter with some thoughts on setting your own personal investment policy, an essential tool of every serious investor.

Don't think you have to grasp it all after a single reading, because you probably won't. And don't beat yourself up if you don't get it all after two readings. Read this chapter a couple of times, and it will help to put it all in perspective. Then pick up a magazine like *Fortune* or *Money*, or a *Wall Street Journal* or two, and see if what they write makes a bit more sense because of what you read here. I think it will.

Investing in the market for most of us means buying shares of *common stock* in one company or another. So let's start: What is a share of common stock? It's a piece of paper, a certificate actually, that represents a small percentage of ownership of a company, such as General Electric, Microsoft, or Exxon. Only companies that have registered with the U.S. government—the Securities Exchange Commission (SEC) specifically—can sell their shares in the United States. Companies so registered are referred to as public companies, which is shorthand for "companies registered with the SEC whose shares are allowed to be publicly traded." The SEC regulates their stock-selling activities by defining the kind of information they must disclose before they can sell and under what circumstances they can sell.

The SEC also regulates the marketplaces, called exchanges, where these shares are sold—the New York Stock Exchange (NYSE), the National Association of Securities Dealers Automated Quotations (NASDAQ), and the American Stock Exchange (ASE) primarily—and also the less formal arrangements for the shares of much smaller companies. These shares are traded only on systems known as the Bulletin Board and the Pink Sheets. Don't ask; you don't want to go there.

Risk Tolerance: Where You Are in Your Life and How Securities Fit Into It

This is the one area of investing that probably gets more press, good and bad, than anything else. The rise and fall of stock prices, a sure thing on any day the market is open for business, is always exciting to some, frightening to others, and magnetic for still others. As a result, it makes the news, which means almost everyone has an opinion about the stock market, even if that opinion is to stay away from it. And the reality of history, while hard to accept during a deep recession, is that owning marketable securities—stock in public companies to be specific—has produced the best investment returns over long periods of time. One often-quoted statistic is the 11% average annual growth of an investment in stocks over the past 75 years (*not including the recent bear market*).

The problem of course is that they may produce huge losses during very short periods of time, as the periods from 2001–2002 and 2008 and early 2009 have amply demonstrated. So every teacher has the same choices that every other American has—go for a slice of that handsome, long-term return or stay away because the volatility is too uncomfortable or too difficult to manage or takes too much study. There's no right or wrong answer here. The only answer is the one that's right for you, hopefully somewhere between the extremes, and this chapter will try to help you understand enough of the investment choices to determine that.

There is one principle that governs all investing, including the stock market, and that is this: The potential reward for making an investment should be commensurate with the potential risk of loss inherent in that investment. If you invest conservatively, you accept lower returns in exchange for taking on lower risk. If you invest aggressively, you are taking on greater risk in the hopes of greater-than-average rewards. Whenever that relationship gets out of balance, there is the opportunity for either financial disaster or really big gains, and often both possibilities exist in close proximity to each other. The bear market of 2008–2009 produced huge losses, and at the bottom, what followed were huge opportunities for profit. The risk always lies in determining where the profits will occur and where losses will continue as the economy sorts itself out.

Most any investment adviser or financial planner will tell you that the closer you are to retirement, the more conservative—read *safe*—should be your investments, because you have fewer years left to catch up if you hit a rough patch. Does that mean that you should swing for the fences early in life? Not necessarily, but maybe.

OK, maybe we need a few more words here. In this chapter, we'll talk about the considerations that you should take into account when deciding about investing in securities, and a very important one is *risk tolerance*. How much risk are you prepared to take? That isn't a function of just how old or young you are, but how you feel about taking risks over which you have no, or very little, control. The market isn't very consoling to those of us who want to control everything in our environment, because it has proven time and again that its direction cannot be predicted with certainty for any length of time. Although there are lots of ways to guess the likelihood that it will go up by $X\%$ or down by $Y\%$, the market often makes the most dedicated followers look silly when it does the exact opposite of what they predicted. So investors in the market need to have some protections in place to enable them to manage the risk to a level at which they feel comfortable. And again, the basic rule of the market is that greater risk is rewarded with the potential for greater gain. Still, with reasonable prudence, investors can realize returns that will comfortably exceed the cost of living or the returns they will realize from most other forms of investment and thus help themselves get ahead of the game.

How Much Pain Will You Accept Along the Way?

Investing in stocks is perhaps akin to being in a competitive, noncontact sport, such as golf or chess. You can spend as much time as you want studying, planning, practicing, and analyzing to make good decisions, and the more of that you do, the higher the likelihood your performance will be better. Yet you can still be in the game with only a fraction of that work—you just accept a greater possibility that your results will be less than they would otherwise be. Happily, the choice is up to you, as long as this isn't the way you intend to make your living and you don't gamble with the rent money.

Discuss your investment strategy with a professional investor or investment adviser, and he or she will likely ask you early, "What is your level of risk tolerance?" The question is one you must ask yourself before you begin a serious investment program of any kind, but it is particularly relevant in more volatile forms of investment, like the stock market. You must determine how much potential for loss is acceptable for you—not comfortable, for no loss is comfortable for most of us, but acceptable—in the search for profit. How to do that is different for most of us, but it's really about the ability to know how you feel when things happen that you didn't expect.

Here's a little self-test that might help: Assume you buy a stock, and it goes up 20% after you buy it, and then it goes down 10%, cutting your profit in half, more or less. If you then think that this is normal behavior—the ups and downs of the market—and you look for it to turn up again, you are within your comfort zone of risk tolerance. If, however, you watch the stock each day and wonder if you should sell to prevent further losses, or you realize you wish you weren't holding the stock at all and would rather forgo the potential profit on this investment rather than having to worry about additional losses, you have exceeded your acceptable risk tolerance.

Investment Strategies Overview

If the opening of this chapter hasn't driven you to bury your money in a hole in the backyard, you may want to consider some investment strategies that you could use to make some of those choices spoken about in the paragraphs above. So let's talk about some of them here. And keep in mind that these are, to some extent, generalizations, with infinite varieties and blends in between. But this will give you a feel for the playing field, so to speak.

The Stock Picker Approach

I enjoy the excitement of the market, and I'm a stock picker. That means I pick individual stocks to buy, for the most part, with minimal investment in other kinds of securities. It also means my portfolio is almost never balanced. What does that mean? It means having your investment cash spread among a variety of investment types, such as stocks in different industries, bonds of different types, real estate, cash, and maybe even collections of art and stuffed teddy bears. The idea is to protect yourself from reversals in one area because you have investments in other areas that aren't being hit at the same time. It's the old don't-leave-all-your-eggs-in-one-basket strategy, and it will be the almost universal advice given to nonprofessional investors, because it lowers the risk.

However, if you see the market as "fun," as I do, you might choose to do your own research or subscribe to investment newsletters or some of the online advisory or research services that abound on the Internet. And unless you have a significant amount of money to invest, your portfolio is likely to be less than balanced, as the professional advisers would define it. I never have more than 10 or 12 stocks in my portfolio, because I can't keep an eye on more than that, and since no one is managing my stocks but me, that is important. Yet there are many more than 10 or 12 sectors from which to choose stocks to buy. *Investors Business Daily*, a well-regarded investment publication, tracks 197 distinct industry groups that they think define the market, with each industry group being made up of companies that are essentially in the same or similar business. The cosmetics/ personal care group includes Avon, Colgate-Palmolive, Herbalife, Kimberly-Clark, and over 40 other mostly smaller companies. So picking a stock involves choosing the kind of business you want to be in, the size of company, and the industry in which the company operates. And that's before you look at the company's individual performance— earnings, sales growth, dividends, and all the rest.

Of course you can either choose to do all that research yourself, poring over annual reports, reports filed by companies with the SEC, newspaper stories, and the like, and draw your own conclusions, or you could use the research gathered by companies that are in that business. Most brokerage firms have extensive research departments to help them find good companies to recommend to their customers, and there are literally hundreds of newsletters written by people who consider themselves experts at doing that analysis and making recommendations in return for your subscription to their newsletter or advisory service. Mark Hulbert (http://store2.marketwatch.com/index1.htm) sells an information service whose sole objective is to help you evaluate which investment newsletters have the best track record, thus helping you to decide which advisers to listen to. Yes, that's an adviser to choose an adviser. It's a very specialized industry, don't you know.

Advisory services range in cost from nothing (provided by the brokerage firm that has your money to invest) to hundreds of dollars a month. I don't have the time or interest to do my own basic research, so I use several research sources to help me find potential investments. My favorites are www.morningstar.com (basic service for free to about $15 a month for their premium service with tons of tools you can use) and www.investors.com (basic service for free to about $30 a month, with an extensive list of information and analysis options that can easily cost thousands of dollars a year for everything). I also use www.marketwatch.com for general information, price charts, and getting email alerts when something is reported to the media that I want to know about (basic service is free). Each of these provides a lot of free information and a lot of premium services for additional fees. I typically use their basic services at low cost, with a minimum of extras.

Another source I greatly respect is Jim Cramer. Some of you may have listened to Jim's radio show or seen him on TV. There is likely no more flamboyant proponent of stock picking on the planet than Jim, and if you can get past the theatrics he's a very smart guy. I highly recommend his latest book, *Getting Back to Even* (Simon & Schuster, 2009), for some very creative ideas that most anyone could use.

How well have I done? In a word, OK. My stock market returns over the past few years have been better than the basic market indexes, but usually not much better. As this book was being written, 2009 was a get-'em-back year for me, with very ample rewards for my good purchases made at the bottom of the market slump. Still, if it weren't a hobby for me, I might just choose an index fund and ride with the market. But where's the fun in that? Remember, this is my choice for me, not my recommendation for you. I always hope to do better next year (*and next year, I will*). So let's look at some concepts and strategies that might become part of your approach to investing.

The Balanced Portfolio Approach

Let's say you don't want to be a stock picker. Your stomach won't take it, your spouse won't take it, or you have other things you'd rather do with your spare time. So as an alternative, you could spread your cash among stocks from a wide number of industry groups in what is referred to as a *balanced portfolio*. This method is based on the assumption that the overall market will gradually move up over time, and you reduce your risk of a particular stock going down at any one time by being invested in stocks from a variety of industries. If one industry group goes down (remember the dot-bomb years at the beginning of this century), you are protected because you had only a small part of your investment stake in that particular industry. Virtually every investment adviser will urge you to follow this approach because of its risk control features.

The flip side of that choice is this: When one group makes a dramatic move up because of major events (think of $4-a-gallon gasoline and the earnings of the oil companies during that period), you won't get the full benefit of that climb because only a small part of your stake is invested there. In fact, the management of this approach requires that you rebalance periodically to ensure that you continue to minimize the risk of a big downside hit. Rebalance? We need some definition here.

Here's what that means: You periodically sell the stocks that have done the best and buy more of the stocks that have done the poorest. The concept is based on the historically valid assumption that stocks don't go up forever, nor do they go down forever. If you are buying good companies, there will be a rotation in the market, and stocks that have done well will not always do that well, so sell them after they've gone up a lot. And by contrast, stocks that have gone down a lot won't continue to go down forever, so you should have more of them when their turn in the market rotation comes along. I know this requires a bit of faith because it says sell your winners and buy more of your losers. Not exactly the kind of thing you want to brag about at the next social gathering of your friends, unless they're also investors or stockbrokers who understand this stuff. But if you're not going to be an avid stock watcher and researcher, this method of modifying both your gains and your losses will keep you out of trouble most of the time, since no one can predict which group will be the next one to go up or down or when that will happen.

The S&P 500 Index Approach

A third alternative, advocated by some experts, including John Bogel, founder of the Vanguard Group of mutual funds and author of *The Little Book of Common Sense Investing,* is to simply buy the entire market or at least the largest part of it. This approach says you simply invest all your cash in a kind of superfund that in turn holds all the stocks in the Standard & Poor's 500—the 500 largest companies traded on U.S. markets. Called the S&P 500 for short, this group represents about 75% of the market value of all U.S.-traded stocks and is, for many purposes, considered to be the proxy for the entire market. Based on thinking somewhat akin to the balanced portfolio approach, you assume the market will over time gradually move up, as it has done in the past, and you just invest your money and forget it. In the future, it will probably be worth more than you paid for it, and probably by more than the mitigating factors of inflation and the cost of living. You will note this approach also requires something of a leap of faith, if you keep in mind that the S&P 500 stood at 1,500 in 2000, dropped to 800 in 2003, rose again to 1,500 in 2007, only to fall to 700 by the beginning of 2009.

Types of Companies You Might Choose to Invest In

Growth Stocks Versus Value Stocks

Growth companies are assumed to be fast growing as a principal strategy either because they're in a growth industry—for example, Internet marketing, digital media, electronic gaming, and so on—or because they're young or small and selling into a very large market—for example, handheld computing; think iPod. These companies will command relatively high prices because the assumption is they will grow sales and earnings and will therefore be worth more in the future than companies that are growing more modestly or not at all. They will typically increase in price in anticipation of that rapid growth, because more investors want in on their success. Of course when their growth stalls or is less than expected, the reaction can create big drops in their market price as disappointed investors unload shares.

Value companies are thought of as being more stable—think of the largest companies in the world today, names we readily recognize and think highly of—General Electric, Microsoft, Boeing, Walt Disney, Wal-Mart, and so on. These companies are not going to grow like rockets, but they're not going to fade away either. Money invested in these companies is relatively protected from wide swings in price that typically mark the path of growth companies. They are thought to climb less fast, but they drop less severely when they disappoint. This has historically been the case despite the notable exceptions that occurred in the bear market of 2008–2009, in which some of these companies saw their share prices drop to less than $10 a share.

In planning your investment horizon (how far you are thinking in terms of time frame to earn the desired return), you might consider Table 9.1.

Table 9.1 Choosing Between Growth and Value Stocks

	Short-Term Investment[a]	Long-Term Investment[b]
Growth stocks	Yes	Yes
Value stocks	Not so much	Yes

a. periods of 1 year or less

b. periods longer than 1 year

The point of this little table is to suggest that value stocks should not normally be considered for short-term investing, because their very nature implies the greatest return comes from giving them time to gradually produce results while minimizing the swings in price that may befall other companies in the short term. Slow and steady wins the race—isn't that from some tortoise-and-hare story? But remember—it was a long race, not a sprint.

Large-Cap, Mid-Cap, and Small-Cap Stocks

You will also hear stocks referred to by the size of the company, and this too is important information to consider in deciding which company's stock you want to own. *Large cap* (or large capitalization) means a company with a total market value, as measured by the price of its common stock times the number of shares of common stock owned by all its stockholders, of $5 billion or more, in general. *Mid-cap* stocks are generally considered to be those with a total market value of $1 billion to $5 billion, and *small-cap* stocks are those with a total market value below that. Why does that matter? Because the large-cap companies are considered sturdier and less likely to get into trouble, while the small-cap stocks are more likely to grow more rapidly (which also means their share prices are likely to grow more rapidly) and also get into trouble more readily, lacking the resources of larger companies (which also means their share prices are likely to fall more rapidly). Take a look at Table 9.2.

Table 9.2   Large-, Mid-, and Small-Cap Stocks: Size Versus Expectations

	Large Cap	Mid Cap	Small Cap
Size of market value, approximately	$5 billion and up	$1 billion to $5 billion	Under $1 billion
General perception of growth prospects	Low	Medium	High
General perception of risk	Low	Medium	High
Likely to be a growth company	Low	Medium	High
Likely to be a value company	High	Medium	Low

Hold 'Em or Fold 'Em:
Short Term Versus Long Term

We can call anyone who buys stocks an investor, but in reality, that's something of a misnomer. An investor is the name applied to someone who buys a stock for a relatively long period of time, typically a year or more, with the thought of giving the company time for their strategies to bear fruit in terms of earnings, which in turn will raise the price of their stock. But there are lots of people who buy stocks for much shorter periods of time, with planned holding periods from a few months to a few hours. These folks are usually called traders—except in the *Wall Street Journal*, where everyone who buys stock is called an investor. Traders are not usually interested in giving the company time to manifest its success in the price of the stock. They are more likely to be buying because they think others will be buying, which will drive the price of the stock up, or they think others will be selling, driving the stock price down. Their objective is to get in at the start of that activity and to get out at the end of it, regardless of what's actually happening to the company itself. I have been both a trader and an investor over the past few years, and I can't tell you from my experience which is more rewarding, but I'm clear that trading is more fun. Then again I have a pretty high tolerance for pain, ah, risk.

As you might imagine, these two types of buyers look at different kinds of information to guide their decisions. The investors will typically look at how the company's doing—earnings history and prospects, sales history and prospects, market potential for their products, new developments in research and development, and so forth. These things drive the future value of companies and can be grouped together as *fundamental* tools of analysis, or fundamentals for short.

The traders, by contrast, don't want to wait around for the company to deliver. They're more interested in acting based on the market's anticipation of those company developments—what other buyers and sellers think will happen to the company's stock when those developments materialize. That information is best gained by watching what those other buyers and sellers are doing based on their expectations, and that is visible by watching their buy and sell transactions. Those transactions are tracked and reported every minute of every market day by the stock exchanges where such transactions are carried out, with a dizzying array of statistics and charts that measure stock price movement by the minute, the number of shares that are traded each minute, the amount of volatility that the market is demonstrating at any given moment, percentages up and down, and on and on and on. This is called *technical* analysis, and it is the basic tool of the trader, especially the very short-term trader. The belief, supported by years of, you guessed it, statistics, shows that price and volume movements will follow certain patterns that can be recognized and predicted with some degree of reliability. This would be a cinch if that degree of reliability were consistently high or even consistently anything. But it's not, and so the most successful traders, and many investors as well, use a combination of fundamental and technical tools to make buy and sell decisions. So here's another little chart—Table 9.3.

Table 9.3	When to Use Fundamental Versus Technical Analysis	
Technique to Use	**Short-Term Investment**[a]	**Long-Term Investment**[b]
Fundamental analysis	Not so much	Yes
Technical analysis	Yes	Not so much

a. periods of 1 year or less

b. periods longer than 1 year

Stock buyers who intend to keep their holdings for a few hours (the *day trader*), a few days, or a few weeks will invariably rely primarily on technical analysis for their buy and sell decisions. The longer the planned holding period, the more likely the traders will begin to act more like investors and use both forms of analysis or perhaps only fundamental analysis, if they are prepared to disregard the minor movements in a stock over the short term.

SUMMARY OF KEY IDEAS FOR CHAPTER 9

1. Your investment strategy must be driven, first and foremost, by your tolerance for risk. If you take risks that are uncomfortable, the inevitable losses, besides being painful, become reasons for self-doubt and fear, inappropriate feelings for any investment activity.

2. Decide if you want to be a stock picker, a balanced portfolio investor, or an S&P 500 index investor. That one choice defines at a fundamental level every other stock market decision you will make.

3. Various kinds of companies become appropriate investment options at various stages of the market. Growth versus value and large cap versus mid cap versus small cap are not lifelong choices but choices based on your investment policy and the state of the market.

4. The two principal methods of choosing which stock to buy are called fundamental analysis and technical analysis. Fundamental analysis focuses on the inherent strength of the company; technical analysis focuses primarily on timing—when to buy and when to sell. Serious investors use both methods.

10

Other Ways to Own Companies

(Besides Starting Your Own)

Other Equity Choices

In addition to common stock, there are lots of ways to participate in the securities markets these days, as a result of very creative people on Wall Street finding new ways to sell us something. Let's take a few paragraphs to describe the most common ones.

When it comes to equities, owning a piece of an operating company, there are four basic forms of ownership. One is direct—buy shares of stock in a specific company. The others are indirect—buying shares in a pool of stocks that includes the company or companies you want to own. There are lots of variations, but this section will give you a start on understanding the language, which is a prime objective of this book. So let's define each of these at the risk of providing too much detail for some and too little for others.

Preferred Stocks

Many companies that issue common stock also issue a different ownership interest called *preferred stock,* a hybrid form of ownership that has some features of ownership and some features of debt. Many companies offer both common and preferred shares to the public, and both will fluctuate with the movements in the market, although preferred shares usually are less volatile because they typically have fixed dividend requirements—such as 6% of their face value or $10 per share—that must be paid before the company can pay dividends on the common stock. That feature of a guaranteed return is the debt characteristic that gives preferred shares more price stability than common shares.

There is one other advantage that preferred shares have because of their debt characteristics. It's how they got the name *preferred,* and it has to do with the legal priority of distributing the remaining assets of a company that stops doing business and liquidates itself—think of Circuit City or Mervyn's, two companies that recently ceased operations. In such situations, there is usually not enough money after selling all the assets for everyone who invested in the company to get their money back, so the law defines who gets first payment and who gets last payment, if there's anything left. Creditors get first payment—people the company owed money to. Then come the preferred shareholders—they are *preferred* in liquidation to the common shareholders, who get what's left, if anything. In the spring of 2009, American car manufacturers were selling for a couple dollars a share because everyone worried that their common stock would soon be worth nothing if there were a shutdown of operations.

Preferred shares are a way to participate in the success of a company without taking on a full share of the risk. As for volatility, preferred shares rise less rapidly in price than common shares because their owners don't typically get anything more in payment for their investment than the stated dividend, regardless of how well the company does. These shares also fall less rapidly because of the preferred protections built into them.

In a final attempt to muddy the waters for you, it might be useful to know that many preferred shares issued today are convertible into common shares at the option of the shareholders, thus giving them a chance to opt in for the rewards, and the risks, of common stock ownership. Convertible preferred shares will demonstrate volatility somewhere between pure preferred shares and common shares, depending on the fortunes of the company.

Mutual Funds

When most people think of investing without actually buying shares in individual companies, they typically think of mutual funds, which have been around for many years in various forms. When you buy shares in a mutual fund, you are buying an interest in a financial company that, in turn, takes your money and the money of many others and buys shares of stock in a variety of companies. They then manage those investments, buying and selling as they think appropriate, hoping to produce an increase in the value of the shares of the mutual fund company, the shares you bought. You can probably find a mutual fund that will target just about any market sector that grabs your fancy, as there are over 23,000[1] of them today.

The variety of the thousands of mutual funds that exist today is the result of investors wanting to own certain kinds of companies. You can, for example, buy shares in a mutual fund that buys only common stock of energy companies or financial companies or American companies or European companies or large, stable companies or small-growth companies. The value of the mutual fund shares rise and fall based on the collective value of their holdings, which is recalculated daily and is called *net asset value.* The price at which mutual fund shares are bought and sold (or redeemed) is almost always based on the net asset value of the underlying stocks at the end of each day. In fact, you can only buy a mutual fund based on the net asset value at the end of the day that you made your purchase. So you can't know the price per share that you paid until then. Thus mutual fund shares are usually purchased by ordering a dollar amount to be invested, and the mutual fund company will calculate their ending net asset value and credit your account with however many shares your total investment will buy. Thereafter, your shares are valued daily at the net asset value for that day.

A key thing to remember about mutual funds is that some charge a sales commission, or *load,* when you purchase their shares. That load, which can be 4% to 6%, effectively reduces the amount of money you will actually be investing.

🔑 KEY POINT

It's good to know that there are many mutual funds that don't charge a commission—called *no-load* funds—in which all of your money is put to work, instead of 95% of it. Morningstar tracks over 9,300 no-load funds, so there are lots of choices.

Regardless of a fund's load or no-load characteristics, all mutual funds charge operating fees to compensate the fund managers for the costs of managing the fund, and that amount, ranging from perhaps

---

1. Morningstar tracks 23,454 mutual funds as of last count.

.5% to 2% or more annually, will reduce your net return. So when you go shopping for a mutual fund, here are two key questions to ask:

- What is the commission, or load? Is it charged when the purchase is made or when the shares are sold back or redeemed later? Whenever possible, choose a no-load fund unless you really believe the load fund is much better.
- What is the annual *expense ratio*—the management fee—as a percentage of the money invested? There are lots of good funds with expense ratios less than 1% a year, a good metric to shoot for.

There are lots of other questions to ask when considering a mutual fund investment that we can't cover here, but the best source I know of for information about mutual funds is the company most often quoted for its objectivity in evaluating mutual funds, Morningstar. Their website (www.morningstar.com) offers tons of information to help you make choices. Much of it is free, and all of it is available for about $15 a month. For example, they have a great method of helping you visualize the kind of stocks an individual mutual fund holds. The visual looks something like this:

	Value	Blend	Growth
Large cap			
Mid cap			
Small cap			

The concept of the visual is that virtually every mutual fund can be placed in one of the boxes in the grid, based on the kinds of stocks its managers invest in, which in turn is based on their intended investment strategy. The shading in the center of this example indicates that the fund being represented is one that buys stocks that are mid cap in size and that its portfolio holds a fairly equal mix of growth and value stocks, thus its results would be expected to be a blend of the two. Virtually every mutual fund Morningstar tracks can be categorized this way, even if some of the fund managers may stray slightly from their investment strategy from time to time.

Exchange Traded Funds

A form of security that has only been around for a few years, exchange traded funds (ETFs) have grown dramatically in acceptance because of the lower cost of investing in them. There are over 800 ETFs available today, and more being launched every year, with much the same variety of choices as with mutual funds. An ETF is a basket of stocks much like a mutual fund, except for several important differences.

First, it is not actively managed like a mutual fund. The company offering an ETF doesn't have people looking for the right time to buy or sell the underlying shares, because the ETF is designed to hold a certain fixed list of company stocks—for example, 50 specific technology stocks or 30 energy companies or 20 China-based companies. Every dollar the ETF managers receive goes into the same basket of securities without regard to the movement of stock prices in the underlying companies. However, the price of an ETF share is subject to more market influences than a mutual fund share, and the market price may or may not resemble the net asset value of the underlying securities.

Second, ETFs are traded like individual stocks. They are valued moment by moment during the trading hours of the markets, as opposed to mutual funds, which can only be valued or traded at the end of the day. Thus an ETF can be bought and sold anytime during a market day, and you will know the exact price per share you are paying, while the mutual fund's price will only be available at the end of each trading day. On the downside, you pay a commission for trades in ETFs, as you do with stocks and unlike no-load mutual funds.

Third, because of the less active management compared to mutual funds, the expense ratio is much less than mutual funds, with most ranging from .07% to .20% annually. This makes your invested capital more valuable, because more of it is kept invested as long as you own your shares.

Fourth, and this is a caveat, because these shares are not actively managed like mutual funds, they may have more volatility than mutual fund shares with a similar focus, and the fund manager can't sell the share of a component of the fund that is in trouble, as a mutual fund manager might.

Index Funds

At the low end of volatility and also of active management are index funds. An index fund management team invests in the securities of the underlying index they are trying to emulate, and the fund share price moves with the market value movements of its underlying securities, just like a mutual fund or ETF. The principal difference is its breadth. The classic example of an index fund is also the original index fund—the Vanguard S&P 500 Fund, discussed previously as a balanced portfolio approach. There are now at least a dozen competing funds with the same goal of tracking the S&P 500, plus dozens of others that track the Dow Jones Industrial Index, while there are now over 700 index funds of various kinds tracked by Morningstar.

When you buy an index fund share, you are buying a share in all the underlying stocks in the index it represents, and your investment will move along with the underlying index. The rationale for this type of investment, as noted previously, is that the market over time moves gradually upward as the economy prospers over time. Fluctuations in individual stocks are flattened out by the breadth of the index, and management of the component stocks is not an issue, because there is none. Thus, say the proponents, the investor can in effect put his or her money away and forget about it while the economy allows it to grow over time. While unquestionably less volatile than individual stocks, the market results of 2007–2009 will not give many comfort that a buy-and-hold strategy is a good idea indefinitely.

Bonds: The Safety of Fixed Income

For those who prefer to avoid the excitement of the stock market but still want to participate in the market's income-producing opportunities, bonds are a viable option, and nearly all financial advisers will recommend that investors have at least some of their investment money in bonds as a diversification strategy for a balanced portfolio. A bond is simply a note payable to you for money that you have effectively loaned to a public company for use in their business. You may not have loaned that money directly, but someone did when the bonds were first issued, and when you buy a bond, you effectively take over that original lender's position, with rights to the payment of interest and, ultimately, the principal of the bond. Bonds can be purchased and held until maturity, meaning the date the issuing company has promised to repay the loan, or you can sell them on the open market just like a share of stock.

Lots of Varieties, Lots of Choices

If you thought the choices and options in stocks were confusing, you may not find much comfort in bonds, also called fixed-income investments because they pay a fixed amount of money—interest—at regular intervals. There are lots of choices here, too, but much less information to help you make those choices. Let's see, there are bonds issued by U.S. companies and foreign companies (*corporate bonds*), by state and local governments (*municipal bonds*), by the U.S. government (*treasury bonds*), and by foreign governments as well. All have different levels of risk, and a variety of special terms that may, for example,

- allow the company to redeem or pay off their bonds early, thus saving interest that they would otherwise have paid you ("callable");
- allow you to convert their bonds to shares of their stock, allowing you to potentially earn added gains from the company's success in return for forgoing future interest income ("convertible");
- carry insurance to guarantee to you that they will never default on their commitments, as long as their insurance company survives ("insured");
- sell at a deep discount but pay no interest at all until maturity ("zero coupon bonds").

To help your sense of safety, credit rating companies—Standard & Poor's, Moody's, and a few others—assign quality ratings to bonds to help investors sort out the best investments, called *investment grade,* from the less than best, called *speculative grade.* At least 10 rating levels are used for various issues, ranging from AAA at the top (investment grade and probably insured) to D at the bottom (already in default on interest payments). Bonds rated BBB or above are considered investment grade, and those rated below are considered speculative. If you want to get the rating for a bond you are interested in, you can register for free at www.moodys.com and look up ratings for thousands of issues.

All this is an attempt to measure the risk of default, the possibility that the issuer of a bond may at some time in the future be unable to make the interest payments or retire the bond when it matures. If your risk tolerance is low, you buy AAA issues; if you're swinging for the fences, you buy B or C issues and hope for the best while earning larger interest payments because of the greater risk. As for web-based information resources, there is www.investinginbonds.com and probably others as well.

Sounds simple enough, and there's not so much daily excitement wondering what the market is doing.

Well, not quite. There are some wrinkles to know about here, too, as not everything is fixed in the world of fixed-income investments.

Consider this example: You buy a bond issued by General Dynamics Corporation paying 6% per year. If you bought that bond when it was first issued for $1,000 (the typical face value of a bond) you will be paid $30 every 6 months for as long as you hold the bond, until General Dynamics redeems it at maturity by repaying you $1,000. Since most bonds are issued for long periods of time, say 10 to 30 years, that would be a stream of income you could count on as long as General Dynamics is in business.

However, if you want to sell the bond before its maturity, you could sell it on the market just like a stock. But let's say that when you want to sell it, time has passed, interest rates have generally increased, and comparable bonds are paying 8% a year in interest, or $80. Investors would have the choice of paying you $1,000 for your 6% bond or buying some other company's 8% bond for $1,000. Which choice do you think they will make? Good guess—they'll buy the other one because it pays more. Now, let's suppose you're committed to selling your bond. If you cut the price of yours, you might still be able to sell it. In fact, if you offer to sell your bond for $750 instead of $1,000, a buyer could choose between a $1,000 bond that pays $80, or 8%, or your $750 bond that pays $60, also 8%. You can now sell your bond, but you'll not get the same amount you paid for it because interest rates are higher now, and your 6% bond is worth less to a potential investor as a result.

And that's what the securities market for bonds will reflect also. As a result, bond prices fluctuate largely as a function of the current state of interest rates compared to their official *coupon rate*. As interest rates rise, bond prices generally fall, and as interest rates fall, the reverse is true. So the trick to understanding bond prices is to know that when the effective interest rate or *yield* falls, bond prices rise. Conversely, when interest rates rise, bond prices fall.

Junk Bonds: The Exceptions That Prove the Rule

But there are exceptions. Aren't there always? The most notable exceptions occur when there is some question as to whether the issuing company is going to be in business when the bond matures, and that risk factor will typically lower the market price of their bond by more than the interest rate differential alone would do. When you throw into the mix the quality of the company, you get another element that affects price, the most vivid examples of which are bonds typically referred to as *high-yield bonds* or *junk bonds*.

Because of the wide range of quality ratings, there aren't just investment-grade or speculative-grade or junk bonds. All bonds fall on the spectrum from AAA to D, and when markets are abnormal as they were in 2009, some very highly rated bonds can still pay excellent returns.

These lower-rated securities often pay much higher rates of return than those issued by stronger companies because of the perceived risk of default. As we have learned over the years, junk bonds can be issued by well-thought-of companies. In 1989, the bonds of Western Union, then the world leader in money transfers, were yielding a return of nearly 20%[2] as the company struggled with its debts. Bondholders lost virtually everything over the next 4 years as numerous reorganization attempts resulted in bankruptcy and the disappearance of Western Union as an independent company for quite a few years. I know this because I was one of those bondholders. More recently, in March 2009,[3] the government announced that General Motors and Chrysler—both major issuers of bonds—might have to significantly dilute the interests of their equity stockholders and cancel much of the debts to their bond-holders in order to get continued government bailout support. Higher risk, higher reward—the theoretical mantra of the market. Subsequently, both companies were thrown into bankruptcy.

Buying individual bonds doesn't sound so safe now, does it? Well, if you don't want to pick the individual issues, there are mutual funds and ETFs that focus on bonds exclusively, and some of them are paying handsome yields in relation to their risk, by historical standards. *Fortune Magazine* wrote in its December 22, 2008, issue of several bond mutual funds that were earning high returns as a result of the lending crisis, and while those yields will likely be smaller by the time you read this, the funds are well worth looking at.[4] *Fortune* cited ETF iShares iBoxx $ Investment Grade Corporate (LQD), which was then paying 7.3% for a portfolio of blue-chip companies, and T. Rowe Price's Corporate Income Mutual Fund (PRPIX), which invests in the lower end of investment-grade bonds and was then paying 8.2%. Both funds included large banks in their holdings, which accounted for much of the fear that lowered prices and raised returns, and by February 2009, the slackening of fear had adjusted the returns on these funds to 5.8% and 6.16%, respectively. Buying the actively managed funds instead of the individual bonds will lower your risk, but not remove it, unfortunately. Wouldn't that be nice?

2. *New York Times,* March 22, 1990, "Western Union's Debts May Force Bankruptcy" (http://www.nytimes.com/1990/03/22/business/western-union-s-debts-may-force-bankruptcy.html).

3. *New York Times,* March 30, 2009, "U.S. Lays Down Terms for Auto Bailout," (http://www.nytimes.com/2009/03/30/business/30auto.html).

4. *Fortune,* December 12, 2008, "The Case for Bonds," p. 47.

Government-Issued Bonds: The Ultimate Safe Haven?

One more example of this risk–reward relationship is the choice to buy bonds issued by a company or bonds issued by a government—a state or municipal bond or bonds issued by the U.S. Treasury to finance the federal government. While income tax exemption affects the returns on state and federal bonds, in general, these bonds pay less interest than corporate bonds, because government securities are perceived as safer than any company bond. The presumed safest securities in the world are bonds issued by the U.S. Treasury and backed by the "full faith and credit of the United States." To bolster that idea at the state and local level, many state and local governments buy insurance on their bonds to enable them to lower the rate of interest they pay. A large insurance company will guarantee the government issuer that they will pay the interest or principal if at any time before the bonds are retired, the government issuer is unable to pay. This usually results in the highest rating for safety and, therefore, the lowest interest rate paid by the issuing agency, which lowers government expenses and, of course, the investors' returns. Because of the cost of such insurance, when offset against the savings from lower interest rates, some government agencies issue bonds without such protection. A recent issue by Ramapo College in New Jersey[5] was assigned an A3 rating (about 5 steps below AAA) by Moody's as a reflection of investment grade, but not without some risk.

Does that make all government bonds ironclad? Not so much, as the world financial crisis and credit crunch have impacted state and local governments that routinely borrow to finance their operations while awaiting tax revenues or to build or maintain infrastructure. California's recent budget problems are a dramatic example of the reality that even governments can potentially default on their obligations. Of course most of the time that doesn't happen, and the politicians find a way out, but local governments have been known to default on rare occasion,[6] and recently, state and local governments have been unable to easily obtain insurance for new issues, because of either their difficulties or the financial problems of the insurance companies that normally underwrite such policies. Having said all that, bonds issued by governments across the United States have traditionally and statistically been a safe way to invest, occasional defaults aside.

---

5. Moodys.com, Moody's Investor Service March 27, 2009, press release.

6. The most infamous default cases involving general obligation bonds include New York City's default in 1975 and Cleveland's in 1978.

There is one other category of government bonds mentioned above but not discussed here, and that is the bonds issued by a government outside the United States. Because there are very different issues of risk, currency exchange, and so forth, once you venture outside the United States, that discussion is beyond the scope of this book.

When to Consider Bonds and How Much to Buy

Every portfolio of investment securities should contain some element of fixed income as a hedge against stock market declines. This is the universal advice that investment advisers offer as a fundamental of diversified portfolio management, because it works to lower your risk (which is why every expert recommends it). The trick is to know how much of your portfolio should be in fixed-income investments, and that gets back to your risk tolerance as well as where you are in your life. If you are relatively young and willing to take more-than-average risk for more-than-average rewards, you might have only 10% of your investment assets in bonds. If you are approaching retirement and dependent on this investment pool in the next few years, or if your children's college fund will be needed in the next few years, you might want 90% of your assets in investment-grade bonds. Where you fall in between is up to you and your advisers to determine. The point is to ensure that fixed-income investments such as bonds are a part of your diversification plan.

Buy, Sell, or Hold? How to Decide When and How Much

Well, that's what it's all about, isn't it? If you buy at the bottom and sell at the top, teaching could very soon become an avocation that you do because you love it, not because you need the money. Wouldn't that be sweet?

OK, time to wake up now. In the real world, we achieve something less than the ideal. Not to say we can't get exceptional returns from our securities investments, but let's just make sure we know that always getting the bottom price when we buy and the top price when we sell is not possible. The reasons are varied, none of which have to do with your talent or dedication or even the quality of your research. You'll recall that it often takes months before the National Bureau of

Economic Research declares that we're in or out of a recession—the 2007–2009 recession was officially declared in November 2008, and we were then told that we had been in a recession since December 2007, a year earlier. And they're the experts. So why does it take so long? Because an event often has to be judged on the basis of what happens *after* the event. A stock price has bottomed out when it doesn't go any lower, which you can only be sure of when it, in fact, doesn't go lower later.

Not very helpful, is it?

Actually it is. You just have to accept that getting most of the difference between the lowest and the highest is good enough, and I assure you that will be more than enough to make you very rich if you can do it consistently, which you probably can't, incidentally. But if you can do it most of the time, that will be more than good enough to still achieve the status of successful investor. And that should be your goal. But maybe we can go just a bit further in offering some food for thought on this subject.

When to Buy

- For an individual stock: When you have a strong feeling that the company is about to enter a strong period of good performance, earnings growth, or expansion, and they are managed well enough to pull it off, and you understand their business well enough to even have an opinion about those things, and the overall market seems to be going up rather than down, that would probably be a good time to buy.
- For a mutual fund or ETF: When you feel the past performance of the fund is likely to continue, the managers who make the decisions are seasoned and still there (Morningstar is the best source for this stuff), and the kinds of things they invest in are consistent with the kinds of companies you want to invest in, and the overall market seems to be going up rather than down, buying is worth considering.
- For an index fund: When the kinds of things they invest in are consistent with the kinds of companies you want to invest in, and the overall market seems to be going up rather than down, buying is worth considering. *(These are not redundancies or typing errors—there is a pattern here that you should always have in mind.)*
- For a bond: When interest rates are high in relation to historical rates, buying a bond will give you a high return in the form of

interest plus some price appreciation later if interest rates head down toward more normal levels. When that happens, the price of bonds typically goes up. When stocks are high, interest rate returns need to increase to attract investor money, so bond interest rates tend to be high as well, meaning bond purchase prices are low.

When to Sell

This is the hardest part of any investment program, in my experience. When something we own goes up in price, we want to keep it in the hopes it will continue to go up. When it goes down, we want to keep it in the hopes it will soon turn around and justify our purchase by recovering what was lost and going on to become a profitable purchase. So I guess we should never sell anything, since that about covers all the possibilities. The reality, however, is a bit less simplistic and requires a lot more discipline.

Investors.com, in its voluminous educational material for investors, offers a few rules worth considering:

1. Sell whenever your investment has fallen 7% to 8% below what you paid for it, no matter what else you think. The point here is preserving your capital at all costs, so you can invest again later.

2. Whenever anything you own has gone up 20% or more within a few weeks, sell it now, because short-term investors are soon going to sell enough of it to force its price below where it is now, and you'll have to wait much longer to get this price again.

3. When the stock you hold has reached the price you wanted when you bought it, sell it and call it a successful investment. Then decide with cash in hand what to invest in next.

I don't suggest you adopt those rules without question, but I do suggest that you adopt some kind of rules—before you buy—that you will use as the alarm that will trigger a sell order. If you wait until the event has happened to decide what to do that day, your emotions are very likely to get in the way of a good decision. I speak from personal experience. Make the decision ahead of time, and simply let the market tell you when to act on that decision.

A final thought: You should sell a security when your feelings tell you that you are more concerned about it going down than anticipating it going up. That is my definition of worry, and when you are worried about your investments, you have gone beyond the boundaries of your risk tolerance, and you should convert your holdings into cash until you are again anticipating the positive side of stock investing.

When to Hold

Well, that covers when to buy and when to sell. What about when to hold? The answer in my mind is this: There is *never* an investment that should *never* be sold. There is always a time to buy and a time to sell. In between, you hold. But don't let anyone tell you that you never sell. Even Warren Buffet sells sometimes, and so should you.

Your Personal Investment Policy

Here's a key tip on developing your investment strategy that will really help you define your risk policy and manage your investment choices. Call it your personal investment policy. Every institution that invests as a matter of policy has one. Every nonprofit endowment fund has one. You should have one too. Your investment policy should be in writing, and it should contain your thoughts and intentions about things such as

- the goals of your investment program—college for the kids, vacation financing, retirement income, taking care of your parents in later life, and so on;
- the kinds of investments you are willing to make—real estate (including your home), stocks, bonds, savings accounts (*not* including your emergency stash);
- how much of your investment fund you want to have invested in each of these areas.

This doesn't need to be a long document—a page or two may be enough; it just needs to be long enough so that you're clear about what you plan to do. Table 10.1 is a good example of what this might look like. Your goals will change over time as your life proceeds. A

Table 10.1 Our Family Investment Guidelines

Asset Class	Minimum Portfolio Share	Target Portfolio Share	Maximum Portfolio Share
Real estate investments:			
Down payment on our home—not available for anything else. Cash in CDs or money market funds	5%	10%	15%
Total real estate target	5%	10%	15%
Equity investments:			
Large-cap stocks, including ETFs and mutual funds	15%	25%	30%
Mid-cap stocks, including ETFs and mutual funds	10%	15%	30%
Small-cap stocks, including ETFs and mutual funds	0%	5%	10%
International stocks, including ETFs and mutual funds	0%	5%	10%
Total equity target	25%	50%	80%
Bonds and fixed-income investments:			
Short-term maturities—less than 5 years	5%	10%	15%
Intermediate maturities—5 to 10 years	5%	10%	15%
Long-term maturities—greater than 10 years	5%	10%	15%
Total debt target	15%	30%	45%
Cash and cash investments:			
Cash in banks, money market funds and other ready cash	3%	5%	10%
Cash in CDs committed for some period of time	3%	5%	10%
Total cash target	6%	10%	20%
Total all investments		100%	

Our Investment Goals

1. Rent-free living—our first home purchase—down payment of $25,000 needed in 5 years.

2. College for Joey—25% needed in 9 years, then balance spread out over 4 years. Total amount $40,000.

3. College for Jane—25% needed in 12 years, then balance spread out over 4 years. Total amount $50,000.

4. Family vacation to celebrate everyone graduating (and no more college bills)—big trip to Europe for all of us—needed in 16 years. Total amount $15,000.

5. Retirement fund—just for us, with anything left over going to the kids. Amount needed is $10,000 per year for at least 15 years, in addition to what Social Security and our pensions will provide.

primary goal of vacation planning may evolve to a college fund, which may evolve to an emphasis on generating retirement income as you get older, so you should revisit your investment policy every year or two to see if it still represents your current thinking. Your kinds of investments might change after you've become a home-owner, for example, unless you want a bigger and better home down the road. And how much you want to invest in each area will be the most important risk management decision you will make, because it will set your personal asset allocation policy.

For example, using the goals shown in Table 10.1, a couple invest-ing $1,000 a month beginning in Year 1 (in the example, 9 years before college years begin for the kids), continuing that for 15 years, and earning 5% per year on their investments could do the following:

- finance their home down payment in Year 5,
- pay for both of the kids' college education in Years 9 through 15,
- pay for the vacation to Europe in Year 16, and
- have enough left over to finance retirement withdrawals start-ing in Year 17 and going out for another 17 years before the money runs out.

You can't see this in the book because of the limited space on the page, but if you go to the online help tools at www.corwin.com/finan cialmastery, you can see a 50-year template ("Investment Planning for Your Really Important Goals") that will help you decide how much you need to save in order to make it all work.

So when you make your first purchases after you've finished your investment policy, assuming your cash for investment is $10,000, you might invest $6,000 in common stock or mutual funds, $3,000 in corporate or government bonds, and keep the rest in a money market fund as ready cash. Your investment account now has a 60:30:10 allocation, in line with your policy target. Then as you add additional cash to your investment account, additional pur-chases of stocks and bonds would be designed to keep the ratio between those types of investment the same as long as your invest-ment goals don't change.

So how does that help you decide when to buy or sell?

Well, aside from the choices you'll make because a particular security has disappointed you, suppose your common stock that you paid $6,000 for is now worth $8,000. And assume your bonds have not changed in value, maybe because interest rates are stable. Your investment account now valued at $12,000 has an 80:30:10

allocation, which is not what you intended when you established your policy, and that changes your risk for the future. How do you fix that? Here's how: You take your profits on part of the common stock, buy more bonds, and keep more in cash. If you sell $800 of your stock, put $200 more into your money market fund, and buy $600 more in bonds, you will have a portfolio that is $7,200 in stocks, $3,600 in bonds, and $1,200 in cash. You will once again be within your 60:30:10 allocation. Here's what that transition might look like:

Table 10.2 Portfolio Rebalancing Example

	Target ratio	Current market value after gains	Actual ratio as a result	Portfolio adjustments	New market value	New ratio
Stocks	60	$ 8,000	80	(800)	$7,200	60
Bonds	30	3,000	30	600	3,600	30
Cash	10	1,000	10	200	1,200	10
	100	$ 12,000	120	– $	12,000	100

SUMMARY OF KEY IDEAS FOR CHAPTER 10

1. There are several ways to participate in the equity market besides buying common stock of individual companies. One thing they all have in common is that they reduce the risk inherent in buying common stock, usually by diversification or by using debt instead of equity.
   - Preferred stock always has a required fixed-dividend payment, which cushions its price.
   - Mutual funds buy shares in lots of companies, around some theme or goal, and they have professional money managers watching the fund.
   - ETFs and index funds are like mutual funds in their multicompany ownership but unlike mutual funds in that they're not actively managed.
   - Bonds are solely or primarily debt that must be repaid in the future.

2. Bonds are debt certificates issued by some entity that wants to use borrowed money in their operations. Bond issuers include corporations and every level of government. Unlike stocks, which have an indefinite life, every bond has a maturity date when it must be retired or paid off in full.

3. Bonds sell at prices that reflect the perceived risk in owning them, but in a very visible way, by checking the yield, or effective interest rate, the bond is paying. U.S. government bonds pay a much lower rate than junk bonds, reflecting the market's perception of relative risk.

4. Your personal investment policy will help you clarify your goals and risk tolerance and should guide all your investment decisions.

11

Buying Investment Real Estate

Your Home Comes First

One of the realities of building wealth in America is that most of the millionaires in this country made a large part of their fortunes through investing in real estate. As many have learned in the past year or two, that's not as easy as it sounds. Yet I'm pretty sure that none of the millionaires—there were nearly 9 million of them in the United States in 2005, according to CNNMoney.com[1]—would deny the idea that their home is the most important real estate they own. That's not necessarily because it is the best investment you will ever make, although that might turn out to be true, but it will likely be the most important one. So before you consider real estate as a wealth-building tool, reread Chapter 7 and put your home at the top of your list, where you can build wealth and have a safe and comfortable environment for your family at the same time.

So Many Choices, So Little Time

There are five advantages that real estate offers over other investments, and they are variety, scarcity, utility, uniqueness, and leverage. Of the

---

1. http://money.cnn.com/2005/09/28/news/economy/millionaire_survey/index.htm

things that make real estate unlike other investments, truly its strongest selling point is its limited supply. They aren't making any more usable land, so you will always have a one-of-a-kind property, and the location of that piece of property will largely define its value. Real estate is also a comparatively expensive investment—you can buy $500 worth of stock in most any company, but you'll have to add a few zeros before you can buy any kind of real estate, which is why bank lending practices and federal tax policies have had special rules for real estate purchasers.

The golden rule of real estate value, whether you live there or rent it out, is location. A good location will cost more, rent for more, and appreciate more than a poor location. A desirable location will usually be more stable than a less desirable location, barring the widespread real estate bubble of the 2007–2009 variety. The value of an investment in real estate, just like any other investment, is directly related to how valuable others think it is when you want to buy it or sell it. That value is determined by the location of the property, its physical condition, the availability of prospects, and the temperature of the market.

Let's define the various property types, along with some of the most obvious pros and cons of this kind of investing. The following are the kinds of properties most commonly used for investing.

Land

This is a bare piece of ground with no structures on it. It is a speculative investment. A piece of *raw land*, as it's called, does nothing to produce income for the owner. I have a 2.5-acre piece of ground in the desert outside of Los Angeles that I bought from my in-laws many years ago before I knew what I was doing. They are long gone, but the land is still there. I know that because I get a property tax bill every year. There were rumors of airport construction at one time, but the rumors have long since died, even before my in-laws. There is no income, no prospect; no one wants to buy it. Not a great investment. Perhaps my heirs will have better luck. The moral of the story: If you are going to buy raw land, you need to know what you're doing or be prepared to wait until the spread of the population creates enough demand to make it desirable. Should you make land one of your investments, there's some comfort in knowing that the only carrying cost is the property tax bill, as a rule.

My suggestion is to forget it. This is a very difficult investment area for people not knowledgeable in the business of real estate and thus subject to unexpected losses—not a good investment for any but those in the real estate and construction businesses. In the event you are not deterred by my scary words, you might find *The Field Guide to*

Land Investment a useful source, available free at www.realtors.org, a website of the National Association of Realtors. The site is for real estate professionals, so there's lots of free information there for download or reading online. Because it's a respected trade association, the source is reliable, although you might run into some industry language that isn't readily understandable. If that's a problem, look for the educational courses intended for nonprofessionals.

Single-Family Residences

A single-family residence (SFR) is a home like the one you own or want to own. It is a one-dwelling structure to be occupied by one family on a piece of ground that the owner of the house also owns. These can be good investments in the right neighborhoods. They are desirable places to live for renters raising families who, due to their finances or other reasons, don't want to buy a house. They will pay rent to someone who has a house that they can use without taking on a mortgage and all the other responsibilities of ownership.

The good news: When the house is rented, your investment property is 100% occupied. The bad news: When the tenants move out, your investment is 100% vacant and nonincome producing, but the costs of ownership continue until you get it rented again. Also, you are placing a sizeable investment in the hands of strangers, who may not treat it the same way you would if you lived there. Refurbishment after a tenant leaves is one of the most significant costs of investment property ownership, and it speaks volumes about the importance of choosing responsible tenants. SFRs are a good investment if your investment plan is to own two, three, or more of them to spread your risk of vacancies. It's unlikely that all three of your rental houses will be vacant at the same time unless natural disaster occurs. An excellent resource on this area of investing is *Buy and Hold* by Dr. David Schumacher.[2] Get the 2007 edition, not the original.

One more thing: If you don't want to collect rents yourself or get emergency phone calls at 8:00 p.m., you will need a property manager. Read with care the discussion below about property management.

Multifamily Residential Property

This is the technical term for apartments or apartment buildings, any kind of residential property that holds two or more nonowner

---

2. *Buy and Hold: 7 Steps to a Real Estate Fortune,* 2007 edition (paperback) by David Schumacher.

occupants. That could be a duplex (a house with a wall down the middle so that two families can live there without disturbing each other, common in the eastern United States, less so in the west). It could be a 500-unit complex with 10 separate buildings of 50 units each. Residential rentals were easier for me to grasp than other kinds of property, and my first intentional investment was, and still is, a small apartment building in Phoenix, Arizona. I lived in apartments over the years; I understood how they worked, so that felt more comfortable for me. The more units you have under your control, the less you are exposed to the 100% vacancy problem noted previously. Also, apartment refurbishment is typically much less costly per dwelling unit than SFR refurbishment. The downside is that apartment renters are less likely to be long-term renters than people who rent houses, all other things being equal, due to income, family size, employment, the renters' ability to buy a home, and so on.

Oh, and there is one more downside to apartments. It's called *property management*. You can manage it yourself if

- you live within easy driving distance of your investment,
- you're handy with things like plumbing and electricity and appliance repair,
- you have the time to spend on weekends or evenings,
- you don't mind getting those leaking-faucet phone calls at funny hours.

If not, you will need someone to manage it for you who can do those things, so all you have to do is manage the managers. The good news is that every sizeable city has property management companies willing to sell you their management services for a monthly fee of 5% to 10% of the gross rental receipts. The bad news is that some of them are not very good at it. Also, they will typically charge you for their employees doing repairs in addition to the management fee, which can easily cost more than the management fee alone. If you consider that they earn money when they fix something, and they are responsible for deciding what needs fixing, you may get a sense of a little conflict of interest, so integrity is a key ingredient in choosing a management company. I've gone through two in just a few years with my Phoenix building, but I think I'm in good hands now.

Condominiums

Shared ownership of a piece of real estate, they are often called *condos* for short. This is typically residential real estate but can also be commercial property, discussed later. For our purposes in this section, we'll assume we're talking only about residential property. Think of an apartment building where everyone owns their own apartment, but they have shared ownership in the sidewalks and hallways leading to their apartments. This is a tricky form of ownership, so state governments typically have some structural and legal requirements by which companies that build and sell condos must abide.

One of those is the establishment of a legal association and a governing board of owners and directors for purposes of managing the shared-ownership portions of the property—building exteriors, sidewalks, driveways, garages, and grounds, called *common areas*. Another requirement is the payment of monthly dues to the association to pay for maintenance and repair of the common area. Since no one fully owns all aspects of a condo, the rules for shared costs can be quite complex. In California, they are set forth in a lengthy document called the Conditions, Covenants and Restrictions (CC&Rs) that every owner must abide by. Nonpayment of association dues, for example, can result in the association putting a lien on the unit that must be satisfied before the unit can be sold or transferred to another owner, and in some cases this lien may allow the association to file a foreclosure.

As a form of investment, condos have some characteristics of apartments and others of SFRs. You can own a single condo or several, without owning the building, or you can own a building made up of condos. Or a condo can be an unattached townhouse on a shared plot of ground. Remember, the condo is a legal form of ownership, not a definition of the physical form of the property. For example, today I live in a house that sits on half a city lot with a yard in front and a yard in back. The back half of the lot has another stand-alone house sitting on it, and we share a driveway alongside our houses. This is legally a two-unit condo, and my neighbor and I are the association. By contrast, an earlier residence of mine was one apartment in a three-story building of 36 units, itself one of 12 buildings on a 12-acre property. That too was a condo, although they look nothing alike.

As an investment, residential condos are typically more sturdily built and more expensive to own compared to apartments. Yet they are less expensive than SFRs, primarily because with a condo, there is not absolute ownership of all the land and improvements. The principal risks in owning this kind of property, as with apartments or SFRs, are mostly related to the quality of the renter who lives there, cares for the property, and pays the rent. Secondary concerns are the amount of the association dues, the quality of association management, and the location of the property itself.

Commercial Property

An office building or a retail store is a commercial property, a property in which the occupants run a business. This doesn't include the gift basket business your aunt runs from her kitchen. It's a property that is intended to be a business property. Strip malls and shopping centers are good examples of commercial property, as is the office building many of us go to work in every day. Commercial property investing is more complicated than residential investing for several reasons:

- Commercial leases have more complex terms and conditions, such as limitations on subleasing, rental rates based on store sales volume, what the property can be used for, signage on the building, and so on, often requiring the use of an attorney to draft or review an agreement before it's safe to sign it.
- While sometimes rented *as is*, there is often a requirement to modify the property to suit a new lessee, a potentially significant out-of-pocket cost the owner or landlord must bear up front before the flow of rental income begins.
- Typically, longer-term leases (3–5 years), often with multiple renewal options, require a sound sense of what future rental values will be in order to avoid making commitments that end up being below then-current market values.
- Most important, when commercial properties go vacant, they are likely to stay that way for a long time!

If commercial property interests you, and you want to learn more about it than I can cover in this book, check out the "If You Want to Know More" section later in this chapter. In addition, there are many online references and experts willing to sell you their expertise in seminars, CDs, DVDs, and more. I can't knowledgeably recommend any of them, but if you feel comfortable sorting out the wheat from the chaff, it won't take long to find lots of education-for-fee sources.

Industrial Property

A manufacturing or distribution facility such as a warehouse or a factory is typically larger, less well developed, and often less attractive than commercial property. Its purpose is usually for more factory-like, labor-intensive operations than the retail sales or office work that are performed in commercial buildings. Industrial property is less expensive to build than commercial property (often because it can be as simple as four walls and a roof) and less expensive to rent as well. The economic well-being of a community can often be judged by the vacancy rates for industrial property, because a vacant factory means that workers who used to work there don't have jobs anymore.

Investing in industrial property is really better left to experts, in my opinion, because of all the reasons affecting commercial property, *plus* the challenges in determining what constitutes a good tenant (if their business goes bad, they're unlikely to keep paying the rent) and, of course, that other detail—it's either 100% rented or 100% vacant. Again, if you still want to learn more about this kind of investing, read "If You Want to Know More" at the end of this chapter.

The Nature of the Investment and the Returns You Might Expect

As I write this book, my partner and I are trying to take advantage of the tremendous opportunities that exist in residential real estate in Los Angeles County (and elsewhere throughout the country) as a result of the credit crisis of 2008. I looked at a home the day this chapter was written—an SFR—that was taken over by the bank after they foreclosed on the previous owner's mortgage loan. Half of all sales of SFRs during much of 2009 were bank-owned properties as a result of foreclosure, although it's not clear how long that will last. Our challenges in finding a house to buy as an investment involve estimating several things that can't be determined with precision, including the following:

- What price will we have to pay for the property? The bank has an asking price, and depending on the degree of interest, potential buyers could offer more or less than the asking price. Purchase price also carries with it other costs—commissions, closing costs, property taxes, and so on. While most of these are paid by the seller, they will tend to increase the price the seller expects to get for the property.
- How much money will it cost to fix it up so it can be rented or resold? Good values are typically fixer-uppers that need work, and estimating the cost of that work, even when you have a skilled contractor doing the estimating, is risky, with actual costs usually ending up higher than estimates.
- How much will it rent or sell for when it's ready? The rental market is heavily influenced by how many properties are available to rent, and these days there are a lot of them in some areas. The potential resale price is really difficult, since home prices have

been in a free fall for months and are only beginning to show signs of bottoming out, signs that could be months premature.

- How long will it take to get it ready for market? How long will it take to find a good tenant and get it rented? How long will it take for the market to improve enough for us to consider selling it? And probably add several other "how long" questions we haven't thought of yet.

Oh, and that home I looked at as this was being written? It was sold the next day, before we could even make an offer.

So why do it? Because it's an excellent way to build wealth quickly if we do it right, whether the market is expanding or contracting, whether prices are going up or down. Consider the hypothetical example in Table 11.1. For simplicity, the example assumes you have paid for the property and the needed repairs in cash without having to take out a mortgage loan, and you own the property for 1 year before you sell it. Keep in mind that the 1-year holding period is to keep the example simple, not to demonstrate a realistic investment goal.

Table 11.1 Real Estate Investment Return: All-Cash Purchase	
Purchase price	$225,000
Fix-up costs	$25,000
Total amount you have invested	$250,000
Rental rate	$2,000 per month
Operating expenses—property taxes, maintenance	$400 per month
Net cash flow ($2,000 minus $400)	$1,600 per month
Annual return on the investment ($1,600 × 12 months/$250,000)	7.7% per year
Potential selling price	$300,000
Profit on the sale ($300,000 less 8% closing costs, less $250,000 original investment)	$26,000
Return on the money invested from the sale ($26,000/$250,000)	10.4%
Add the monthly cash flow from the rental income alone ($1,600 × 12 months)	$19,200
Total return on investment (ROI) if held for 1 year	$45,200 or 18.1%

The example works just as well for longer holding periods, although the numbers will look different. The key point to keep in mind here is that your return is a combination of your monthly positive cash flow and your profit on the eventual sale. You'll notice that in our example, even if you sold the property for just enough profit to pay the closing costs, in effect a no-profit, no-loss sale, you would still have a profit of $19,200 on the investment, for a 7.7% ROI. The key is ensuring that your monthly result is positive cash flow and not negative cash flow. This will raise the likelihood that the property can be sold at a profit later.

The Power of Leverage

The previous example assumes we don't take out a mortgage on the property but pay for it in cash. That can be important, because you won't have to worry about making the mortgage loan payment while you're waiting to find a good tenant or buyer. If you were to take out a loan, however, you would have less of your own money tied up in the deal, you'd pay some interest to the bank, and your total return percentage would be even higher because you didn't invest the whole purchase price out of your pocket. Stay with me here—this is the good part.

That opportunity to use someone else's money for investing is called *leverage.* Remember your high school physics and the studies of pulleys, where the arrangement of ropes and pulleys gave you more lifting power than you could generate on your own? In real estate investing, we use leverage to multiply the buying power of our capital and thus increase the return on our investment, since the profit on the investment would be the same in any event, except that we pay some interest along the way.

Let me help you appreciate the power of leverage when you make an investment in real estate. Consider the previous example one more time, but this time we'll borrow most of the money from the bank. In fact we'll borrow 80% of the money, a conventional mortgage arrangement, and put only 20% as a down payment. Now let's see what that does to our returns.

Table 11.2	Real Estate Investment Return: Leveraged Purchase
Purchase price	$225,000
Fix-up costs	$25,000
Total amount invested	$250,000
Portion of the investment that we contribute (20% × $250,000)	$50,000
Amount borrowed from a lender—80%	$200,000
Rental rate—same as before	$2,000 per month
Operating expenses—same $400 as before, plus $1,100* loan interest	$1,500 per month
Net cash profit ($2,000 less $1,500 in expenses)	$500 per month
Annual return on the money invested from the rental income alone ($500 × 12 months/$50,000)	12.0% per year
Potential selling price	$300,000
Profit on the sale ($300,000 less 8% closing costs, less $250,000 original investment[a])	$26,000
Return on the money invested from the sale ($26,000/$50,000)	52.0%
Add the monthly cash flow from the rental ($500 × 12 months)	$6,000
Total ROI if held for 1 year	$32,000 or 64.0%

a. Your loan payments would reduce the loan balance to be repaid and increase the net proceeds of the sale by a bit, but that is ignored in this example. Consider it icing on the cake.

And if you don't think $32,000 is as good as $45,200, keep in mind that with leverage, you have put up only $50,000 of your investment kitty. You have kept enough cash in your pocket to do this deal perhaps three or four more times before you've invested all your capital. Of course, this assumes everything works out as you planned, or hoped, and that doesn't always happen. As we discussed in Chapter 10, the balance between risk and reward is always present when you make an investment. Your investment choices are a function of your available capital and your tolerance for risk. The greater the risk you take, the greater the potential reward you should expect to earn. And with the power of leverage at work for you, real estate has proven over time to be the greatest creator of wealth of any form of investment, even stocks.

Shared Investment Methods

Beyond the scope of this book are investment types that involve both real estate and securities. These include real estate investment trusts (REITs), which are like mutual funds for buying, managing, and selling real estate. They have special tax considerations that include avoiding income taxes on their income if they pay out at least 90% of it to their shareholders each year. There are also mutual funds that hold only REITs in their portfolio. If either of these seems like an area you might be interested in, I suggest doing some research online, starting with msn.com's moneycentral.[3] Then you might find some offering documents (prospectuses) for a few REITs and learn some of the fine points of risk and reward before actually making an investment.

Finally, there are tenant-in-common investments, often referred to by investors and promoters as simply "TICs," which are typically large partnerships that sell private partnership interests to investors and then pool the money to make large real estate investments. Their operations are similar to REITs, but their ownership interests are not publicly traded securities and are therefore not as easy to sell as REITs, often requiring investors to keep their money in the pot for 6 to 10 years to allow time for investments to mature.

Your Tax Dollars at Work

Because of the unique nature of real estate, it doesn't suffer a permanent decline in value at some future date, like your car or computer, and it will always be where you put it; banks and other lenders have been willing to allow a great deal of leverage in the purchase of real estate. In addition, there's government banking policy. What else do you know of that you can buy for 10% down (or less) and take 30 years to pay off the balance?

The borrowing-enhanced returns demonstrated above are largely possible because the banking regulations in the United States permit greater leverage on real estate ownership than any other form of lending. Our government has consistently fostered the idea that the American dream of owning your own home is a good idea (yes, that was Chapter 8), and they've set government bank regulatory policy to extend that idea to investment real estate as well by allowing a significant use of leverage in the purchase of rental homes and most other forms of real estate. Thank you, Uncle Sam.

_____

3. http://moneycentral.msn.com/

If You Want to Know More

There are tons of resources for those who want to learn more about real estate investing. Some of the best sources depend on how you like to learn. I like to interact with the knowledge experts in person, so I attend meetings of local real estate clubs that meet in my area, which charge nominal fees and have live speakers who are real estate experts (and who still try to sell you weekend programs, CD sets, and various other products to pay for their time). Look for clubs in your area if you learn best, as I do, through live seminars.

There are also likely to be university classes or university extension classes or perhaps even community college classes, where you can interact with a live expert on real estate investing. Sometimes you can even develop a mentoring relationship with one of these experts— perhaps the best way to accelerate learning and avoid the pitfalls of trial-and-error investing—after reading this book, of course.

If you prefer to read on your time schedule, I'd start first at www.realtors.org again, because it's free with no strings attached. Then you might want to visit sites that are for potential investors, such as www.reiclub.com or www.realestateinvestor.com. This is a rich area for web research, as you'll find, with very little effort. Just keep in mind that all these sites want to sell you a membership, a course, a book, or a consultant. The free stuff is designed to get you to want more—not a bad thing, just web marketing at high volume.

SUMMARY OF KEY IDEAS FOR CHAPTER 11

1. Real estate generally requires a much more substantial investment than the stock market, despite the fact that it gets the same benefit of leverage that your home does—that is, you can borrow most of the purchase price and repay it over 30 years if desired.

2. The principal forms of investment real estate can differ quite dramatically in their risk–reward characteristics. The size of the commitment makes it imperative that you choose with great care the kind of investment you will make.

3. Investment returns on real estate can come primarily from rental income or the profit on selling it. The best investments deliver both.

4. The use of leverage—borrowing part of the purchase price—can substantially increase ROI. It can also increase the ownership risk when you have a required loan payment but no tenant paying rent.

12

Taxes and Tax Planning

Keeping All You Legally Can

Income Taxes: Federal, State, Local

Disclaimer: This is not a tax guide, and even if it were, you should never take advice from a book without verifying the benefit to you with your tax adviser. Did I say never? Yep! Did I say almost never? Nope! Does this apply to all income tax advice? Yep! Are there any exceptions? Nope!

There is a phrase that lawyers and the Internal Revenue Service (IRS) use to distinguish good tax strategy from bad tax strategy: Tax evasion is illegal; tax avoidance is not. Seems like a subtle difference as dictionary definitions go, but it can make a huge difference in your financial life. *To evade taxes is foolish and will likely cost you at some point. To NOT avoid taxes is also foolish and will likely cost you almost immediately.*

Since this book is available to all, including the IRS, we will focus on tax avoidance—and a bit of tax planning—to help you make your dollars stretch.

Income without income tax—is there such a thing? Of course there is. You read about it in Chapter 3 (IRAs, 401(k) plans, FSAs, HRAs, and HSAs), then in Chapter 4 (529 plans), and Chapter 10 (tax-free interest income). And that's just keeping income off your tax return. Deducting money you earn and then spend has the same effect, and that got some attention in Chapter 8 (mortgage interest) and Chapter 11 (investment real estate). So the question is not, can we? The question is, how do we make sure we haven't missed any opportunities?

How the Tax Rates Work

It will help you to understand how the federal (and most state) income tax systems work, so you can see the benefit of sheltering that next dollar of income. Here's the short version.

The United States has a progressive tax system, which means as you earn more, the tax rates get progressively higher. Rates go from 10% to 35%. What does that mean? If you are single and you earn $8,000 in taxable income (numbers rounded for simplicity), you'll pay 10% of that as federal income tax. Remember, this is taxable income after deductions, not *gross income,* and people who earn a gross income of $8,000 likely pay no income tax. So if you earn $30,000 in taxable income instead of $8,000, your tax rate is 15%, *but only on the portion of your income that is above $8,000.* The $8,000 still gets taxed at 10%, and the remaining $22,000 gets the higher 15% rate, giving you a net tax rate of 13.9%, not 15%.

So if your salary as a teacher is $60,000 and your allowable deductions reduce that to $50,000 in *taxable* income, some of that is taxed at 10%, some of it at 15%, and some of it at 25% (the next rate in the progression). The actual calculation would work like Table 12.1.

As this example shows, when people say they're in the 25% tax bracket, they're referring to the highest rate at which their last dollar was taxed, not their effective overall rate, which is always lower because the rates start lower. That's an important tax planning concept to keep in mind for later in this chapter.

Table 12.1 Income Tax Calculation: Without 401(k) Plan or IRA

Income	Tax Rate	Income Tax
8,000	10%	800
34,000 minus 8,000	15%	3,900
50,000 minus 34,000	25%	4,000
Total income tax	17.4% overall	8,700

Now let's suppose you can shelter another $5,000 of your income by taking full advantage of an IRA and your 401(k) plan, for example. Your taxable income drops to $45,000, and your tax bill would be calculated as in Table 12.2.

Table 12.2 Income Tax Calculation: With 401(k) Plan and/or IRA		
Income	Tax Rate	Income Tax
8,000	10%	800
34,000 minus 8,000	15%	3,900
45,000 minus 34,000	25%	2,750
Total income tax	16.5% overall	7,450

As you can see in the two examples, each dollar protected from income tax saves you money at the highest rate you are subject to, thus lowering the average income tax rate on your entire income. So a dollar saved when you're in the 25% tax bracket (called *marginal tax bracket* by your tax preparer) is more important to protect than a dollar when you're in the 15% bracket, because you'll either save or lose 25 cents of it instead of only 15 cents.

So how do you take advantage of your opportunities? Well, you certainly want to take the full deduction for IRAs and 401(k) plans, because every dollar you don't shelter through those options in the year that it's available is lost to you forever.

In addition, the government uses the tax system to favor social purposes that Americans and our legislators believe should be protected, such as those in Table 12.3.

All you have to do in order to get credit for these is to keep decent financial records and prepare a proper tax return. Some social purposes get more favor in some years than others. For example, in 2009 Congress provided for an $8,000 tax credit for first-time home buyers to help them and to help the real estate market for the rest of us. But like so many similar special provisions, it had a limited life, and may already be gone by the time you read this.

As for state income taxes, pretty much everything said about federal income taxes can be said about most of the states as well. Rates are typically progressive, ranging from zero for low-income taxpayers to a high bracket rate of 11% in Hawaii. Rules regarding what you can deduct and what you can't often follow the federal rules, but some states aren't so obliging, and their rules will differ. The concepts of tax

Table 12.3 Your Support Earns Tax Deductions for These Worthy Purposes	
Worthy Social Purpose	**Benefited By**
Real property ownership	Property tax and other deductions
Home ownership	Mortgage interest deduction
Investing in a business	Capital gains tax rates
Supporting charities	Charitable contribution deduction
Keeping healthy	Medical expense deduction
Raising a family	Dependent exemption
Getting educated	Education expense deduction

planning—timing of income and deductions, for example—will work with state income taxes as well, but usually it's best to be guided by federal rules since federal rates are always larger than state rates.

Tax-Planning Strategies

Most of the more sophisticated tax strategies are beyond the scope of this book, but there are some that everyone can take advantage of, if to no other purpose than to postpone a tax bill for a year. Here are a few tips.

- Pay your January mortgage payment in December, early enough so that it shows on your lender's monthly statement. This potentially allows you to use a few hundred to a thousand dollars for another year before Uncle Sam gets it. Remember, there is no requirement that you can deduct only 12 payments a year; you deduct it when you pay it. Same goes for medical bills, charitable contributions, and any other expense for which a tax deduction is allowed.
- If you expect your income to increase next year by enough to push you into the next tax bracket (remember the progressive rate scale), postpone paying your December mortgage payment into January, when the deduction will save you more in taxes. Since this creates the opposite effect of the first tip, you may want to figure your tax both ways to see which saves you the most.

- Sell stocks that you've lost money on before December 22 to ensure you'll get the deduction this year instead of later on. If you still want the stock, buy it back 31 days later, when the price difference is likely to be small, but it will count as a new purchase. If anyone asks, this is the *wash sale* rule.
- If you have a profit on a stock, keep in mind the timing of selling it to capture your profit. If you hold it a year or longer, the tax rate is a flat 15% (5% for low-income taxpayers). If you sell it before holding it for a year, your tax will be the same as your regular tax rate—which could be 25% or more.

Property Tax: Real and Personal

The ownership of real estate—land and buildings—is taxed throughout much of the United States by local governments as a principal means of support for the community services they provide, such as police and fire protection, libraries, and schools. The tax on real estate is called *real property* tax. Business owners also pay a property tax on equipment and furnishings they use in their businesses, called *personal property* by the tax collector.

Real property taxes have long been a point of contention in many communities, perhaps because they are so visible to taxpayers. Also, they can look huge to those who choose to pay them annually rather than as part of their mortgage payments. In California, the amount of tax that can be levied on real property has been limited by law to 1% of the full cash value of the property as a result of Proposition 13, a popular tax revolt in 1978. That equates to about $4.77 per $1,000 of assessed value on average across the state.[1] Property taxes there as a general rule cannot be raised until the property is sold to a new owner or a structure is destroyed and rebuilt. Some say that is a principal reason California's budget is in such chaos, since property tax revenues support the state as well as local government. Not many homeowners say that, though.

I noted earlier that the federal government gives you credit for property taxes to encourage you to own property, because that's the American way. The flip side of that is that local government uses your ownership of property as a way to determine who is best able to support local government services. It may seem like what the feds giveth, the locals taketh away, but it's just one of the ways we redistribute

---

1. http://www.nahb.org/fileUpload_details.aspx?contentTypeID=3&contentID=76984&subContentID=105281

wealth in this country, with the intent that it is for the greater good of all. Besides, the feds don't give it all back, since on an average teacher's salary, you will at best likely get back only 25 cents on each dollar paid to your local agencies.

There's not a whole lot you can do in the way of tax planning for property taxes. You own the property; you pay the taxes. The only exception I know of would involve making significant remodeling to your property, if you live in California where Proposition 13 rules. There are guidelines that determine what constitutes destroying and rebuilding a structure. Too much tearing down during remodeling could cause you to cross the line, so getting professional advice is a good idea before you pick up a hammer.

Filing Tax Returns: Don't Do It Yourself!

When I was much younger and knew "much more," what with an accounting degree and all, I chose to prepare my own income tax returns each year. It was simple when there was just me, my job, and my apartment. Then I acquired in mind-bendingly quick succession a wife, a house, and a family. Suddenly the taxes weren't so simple anymore, especially for a guy working 55-hour weeks during the season when tax returns are filed. You would think a smart professional would pick up on that, wouldn't you? Nope, not until I filed one wrong, missing something that any reasonable, not-personally-involved tax preparer would have caught.

That was the last year I prepared my own return, and I've been grateful for that decision every year since. Today I run a business and a couple of real estate LLCs in addition to the family, home, and so on. I couldn't begin to keep track of all the changes in deductions, allowances, tax forms (in the interest of simplification, of course), and alternative minimum tax calculations—and neither can you, I suspect. So do yourself a favor: Get help.

Getting Help: A CPA or Tax Preparer

There is a pretty large industry devoted to helping people prepare their income tax returns. According to a survey conducted by Tiburon Strategic Advisors, along with several other research and survey groups, in 2002 there were 450,000 certified public accountants (CPAs) in the United States, as well as 40,000 enrolled agents (EAs are generally ex-IRS employees). Of these, nearly all EAs and 170,000 CPAs were in private practice, with tax planning and tax return preparation as their primary revenue source.[2] You can get a simple tax return prepared by H&R Block for around $200 or less. The good news is that it's easy to find a tax preparer. The bad news is that it's easy to get a bad one. Or a lazy one. Or one who follows a memorized or computerized method that ignores your uniqueness. Or one that will always round in favor of the IRS. Or one that will cut so many corners to get you a refund that you may be exposed to serious penalties for underreporting your income.

Did I say at the beginning of this chapter you should always get a professional to help you? At this point, you may wonder what I was thinking. Well, to begin with, I wasn't joking or drinking too much wine as I wrote. You can't do this alone unless that is what you do for a living—and those who teach tax theory and practice at the university level are not excluded, even though they have a leg up on the rest of us. So how do you avoid all the pitfalls of the preceding paragraph? Here are some ways to sort out the bad apples.

Read IRS Tax Tip 2010-06 titled "Eight Tips to Help You Choose a Tax Preparer."[3] The information in this short read is excellent as a starting point.

Interview the prospective preparer before you make a decision. Decide if his or her philosophy is consistent with yours. That doesn't mean hiring someone who believes no one should ever have to pay income taxes—that's the one that can land you in jail. Find someone who thinks conservatively if you want to avoid any risk of audit (but look for the caveat later) or someone who believes in pushing the rules right to the line whenever there is a reasonable interpretation that favors the taxpayer. Both are legal and ethical strategies, but you'll be uncomfortable if you choose the wrong end of the spectrum.

Talk to friends you respect, especially those in the teaching profession, or to financial professionals who know tax professionals as part of their work. Find out who they like and why they like them. If you like what you hear, arrange an interview for yourself. If you know one of those financial professionals well enough, ask him or her to accompany you on the interview so you can compare notes later.

If this sounds like a lot of work, trust me when I say it's worth it. The tax preparer I chose 20+ years ago—Ernest F. Howard, CPA—is still my tax preparer, and I've never regretted that choice. He doesn't always return calls when he should, he doesn't send tax advisories that I'd like to see, and I get occasional political emails as part of his presumed tax

2. http://www.answers.com/topic/tax-return-preparation-services

3. http://www.irs.gov/newsroom/article/0,,id=120129,00.html

avoidance constituency, but he fits my temperament and my risk tolerance boundaries to a T. And if I get an IRS notice that I don't understand, he's on it, and it gets handled. Every time. I've not been audited by the IRS in over 30 years. And that, as they say, is the bottom line.

Tips for Avoiding an IRS Audit

You've filed your return. A year later you get a letter from the IRS. What lousy luck! The IRS audits only about 1% of tax returns filed each year. Not a very large percentage, to be sure, and it seems reasonable to assume that your odds of getting audited once in a hundred years makes you pretty safe in this lifetime. Well, not so fast, you math wizard, you. As it happens, the IRS doesn't pick that 1% of returns at random. Certain factors raise the chances of audit, factors that are surfaced in their review of returns when compared with those same factors in previous years' returns. One factor in your favor—the IRS audits a much higher percentage of returns with incomes over $200,000 than those with lower incomes. That lowers your chances of being selected a bit, and their share of the total audit exposure is actually growing.

What raises your chances of audit? If you work for yourself, file a Schedule C as a sole proprietor, and handle large amounts of cash, you're a likely target. Not you? How about these:

- Taxable income from sources abroad
- Unusually high deductions in relation to your income
- Numbers on your return that don't match those reported by your employer, bank, or mortgage holder
- A tip from an ex-business partner, ex-spouse, or neighbor to the IRS, claiming you are cheating
- Investments in a tax shelter the IRS considers abusive
- Losses reported from a side business the IRS considers a hobby and not a business at all

If the IRS calls, chances are you won't have to actually show up at an IRS office but will be asked to mail them some information to support whatever it is they are challenging. If you get that letter, it's important that you not ignore it. The ostrich approach just leads to more interest and penalties piling up, since the computer doesn't forget. Call your tax preparer and get him or her involved sooner rather than later. You might even break even or come out ahead (but don't count on that last one).

All in all, reasonable care in record keeping and a good tax pre-parer should pretty much insulate you from an IRS audit for almost a hundred years.

SUMMARY OF KEY IDEAS FOR CHAPTER 12

1. Income taxes are the primary way our federal government finances all the services it provides. The IRS is very committed to collecting every tax dollar they can; breaking the rules is called tax evasion, and it comes with nasty penalties.

2. Our income tax system is called a progressive system because the rates get progressively worse as your income grows. This helps to explain why shelter-ing income from tax becomes more important as your salary increases.

3. Legally sheltering your income through the use of retirement plans such as 401(k)s and IRAs saves your income taxes at the highest rate you pay in our progressive system.

4. With a little advance planning, all taxpayers—including teachers—can either lower their tax bill or postpone some of it, often both.

5. Unless you teach income tax law, you should not try to prepare your own income tax return. The reason: You will likely either pay too much, make a mistake, or pay too little in a way that will get caught. Hire a good expert to prepare your return and spend your time making more money.

13

Technology That Can Help You

Earlier in the book, I commented on the fact that my first budget was done entirely by hand on columnar paper with a big eraser. These days, I wouldn't consider such a chore without using some technology tool to make the job easier. Usually it's a software program that helps me organize and capture my thoughts and ideas, like the application, or app, I used to write this book.

We all use technology today in some form, whether an iPod (I actually don't own one), a cell phone (I'm a new smartphone user), or the ubiquitous personal computer (my business has four PCs and an underappreciated Mac). But we learned long ago that it's not the hardware devices that make our life easier; it's the software that we use on that hardware that really makes a difference. I believe that's why IBM doesn't sell personal computers anymore, but they've built a mighty successful business helping their customers use that hardware more effectively.

Still, there are some hardware things to keep in mind before we get into the finance-related software tools. I find even the most tech-savvy users sometimes ignore things that they shouldn't, until they get in trouble. So here are some helpful hints for using the hardware before we get into the software solutions.

1. If it's worth saving the file on your computer, it's worth backing up. If it's worth backing up at all, it's worth backing up whenever you make changes to it. If it's worth backing up

whenever you make changes, and you don't do it with exactly that regularity, you are risking all your data on an event you couldn't imagine happening until it has already happened. And of course at that point, the lesson is learned but painfully so.

My Recommendation: Use some form of automatic backup that works without you having to remember. Even better: Back up automatically to some remote network or online service where the backup is far from your computer and safe from whatever accidents or disasters might afflict your machine. Oh, and keep the access codes safe too, in case you actually need to get to that online backup file some day.

2. When shopping for a new computer, remember that memory and storage space are very inexpensive, so don't scrimp on them. Get all you need up front, because later on, your computer will be thrashing around trying to find space for that last photo (or budget), and you'll wonder why your machine is so slow when it was once so fast. That will happen soon enough without your hastening it by saving a few dollars on memory and storage capacity. How much to get? Memory should be at least 3 to 4 gigabytes, depending on the amount of video or photo material you work with, and storage space should be 100 to 500 gigabytes or more for the same reasons.

3. We're rapidly approaching the era of cordless computing, but we're not there yet in terms of low-cost availability—except for keyboards and mice. Get cordless versions of both. You'll be glad you did, because you can move the keyboard to your lap or a convenient position without tugging at the cord attached to it—same with the mouse.

4. I also recommend the curved, or natural, keyboards, because they keep your wrists at a more natural angle with your arms, and it's more comfortable when you have to spend long hours at the keyboard. It's not medically clear how computer use contributes to carpal tunnel syndrome, but when I'm more comfortable, I feel that I'm more insulated from any possible injuries, whatever the cause. You might also find a trackball mouse more comfortable than a regular mouse, and they require less desk space to operate.

5. Electricity fluctuations occur all the time in some areas, and they can destroy your computer if they get too severe. Invest in

an uninterruptible power supply (UPS) to shelter your machine from power surges. Power strips with surge protectors are similar but not nearly as effective.

Personal Bookkeeping Software

These are applications that keep track of your personal finances on your personal computer. Typically costing $100 or less—often a lot less—their objective is to replace your checkbook and back-of-the-envelope expense tracking with an easier and more accurate way. They are certainly more accurate, although not always easier than that envelope. Some folks feel you need to be an accountant to use these applications, but that's not really so. It just may seem that way if you're not a numbers person. However, the benefits of these programs—keeping track of your finances, giving you reports of spending and budget comparisons, and helping you plan for all kinds of future activities—make them a resource you can't ignore. This chapter can't possibly discuss financial software in any real depth, but I hope to give you enough of a sense of their benefits that you'll be moved to try one, if you haven't already.

Quicken

This is far and away my favorite software application for personal money management. A product of software giant Intuit and selling for $59 to $99, depending on the version, Quicken started out as nothing more than an electronic checkbook, but it's a lot more than that today. Its basic functions are very easy to use, and the capabilities that have been added over the years have only made it better without making it much more challenging to operate. Among the dozens of included features, those I like best include the following:

- Easy reconciliation of all your bank accounts—I used to tell audiences a story about the gyrations I went through to reconcile my checkbook with a pencil and calculator before Quicken arrived. You won't believe how much time this feature alone will save you, and it's always right—every time—as long as you've entered the data correctly.
- Tracking buy and sell transactions in stocks, bonds, and mutual funds—it keeps all the information you need to prepare your tax return at year-end. One drawback: Trying to keep track of

all the small dividends companies pay is more detail than I want to deal with, so I don't.

- Tracking all your credit card transactions—the charges you make and the payments you make—with a few clicks. Of course if you're one of those folks who trusts the credit card company and doesn't track your individual purchases, this won't interest you much. But it should. Especially in this age of identity theft, credit card fraud, and the rest.

- You can enter your budget into the program, and it will print your budget variance reports for you each month. Since it already has your actual expenses, typing in your budget makes it a natural next step to produce the report you'll need to manage that budget.

- If you enter when you are supposed to pay monthly and other regular expenses, it will remind you so you don't forget to pay them on time. I use this one *a lot.*

- It will print checks that you need to give to someone, or you can pay your bills electronically at any one of a list of banks (see the more detailed discussion later about online banking). I almost never write a handwritten check anymore, since printing checks is easier than entering the information two or three times (handwritten check, check register entry, then Quicken data entry).

- You can print a personal financial statement whenever you want one. I see some folks really struggle when they try to get a bank loan and the banker asks them for their personal financial statement. I get mine in three mouse clicks.

- It has several extra little planners build in—depending on what version you buy—for retirement planning, college planning, home-purchase planning, and so on. I've not used these very much, but I love their availability as a reality check.

How Quicken works: You enter your transactions just as you would in your checkbook, including telling it what you spent the money for. For credit cards, it works the same. You don't have to add and subtract to get your running balance, because that is done for you. If you assign your expenses to buckets—called categories—it will put each expense in the specified category. Later on you can easily see every dollar you spent for health care or golf lessons or manicures for any period of time you choose, and the same for everything you've bought from Wal-Mart or Nordstrom's last year. You get graphs and charts of your spending that can help you conceptually see where the money is going, especially if you hate tables of numbers, as my wife does.

Microsoft Money

This product was offered for many years by Microsoft in an effort to take some share of the market from Intuit's Quicken, but to no avail, despite its comparable functionality. Never able to achieve a significant position in the market for personal bookkeeping software, Microsoft announced in 2009 that they would discontinue offering the product and would only support it through 2011. So if you own it now, it will be good for as long as you want to use it, minus the download bank updates that will go away soon. But if you don't own it, don't let someone sell you this one, even for its current $44 price tag. Bye-bye.

Others

The field of personal bookkeeping software is so dominated by Intuit's Quicken that it's virtually impossible to find viable competitors, if you want to compare. I found only one site that had reviews focusing on this category with the appearance of unbiased reporting, and the page where those comparisons were reported is http:// personal-finance-software-review.toptenreviews.com. Since there were lots of ads on the page, I'd proceed with caution even though the reviews seem objective. Names like *Moneydance, AceMoney,* and *BankTree Personal Finance* got pretty good reviews and sell for less than $40, but I've never heard of anyone using these products. My suggestion would be to go with Quicken, but if you want to shop around, this is the site to visit.

Online Bookkeeping Software

With the explosion of bandwidth on the Internet and the proliferation of things we can do online, bookkeeping software was sure to follow, with much of it free, thanks to the benefits of that advertising space on the right side of your screen. Just search for *online bookkeeping software,* and you'll find pages and pages of choices, each seemingly offering effortless bookkeeping and many of them free. I couldn't begin to review them here, but one choice did catch my eye because of its phenomenal growth in a short time.

Mint.com (www.mint.com) is a free bookkeeping application offered only online that has been developed from scratch since 2005, was in beta testing until late 2008 (that means it was still being tested to see if it worked properly), and today has over 1 million users across the country. In a 2009 review by *PC Magazine*, the premier, independent, computer product evaluation publication, the reviewer called Mint.com "the best online personal finance software out there."[1] I took a few minutes to sign onto Mint.com to see if it was as easy to set up and use as the reviewer said. It was. I entered a few pieces of information, *including my bank's security codes*, and it had my bank balances in a minute or so and was ready to do my bookkeeping. The company has bank-grade security to alleviate any concerns about the information I entered, according to the reviewer, so that was sufficiently comforting. Very impressive. So impressive, in fact, that the maker of Quicken bought the company while this book was being written.

This program has tons of features with plans to add more, *and it's still free*. The website for the publisher says they're adding over 3,000 new users a day,[2] so this might be a step up for anyone who considers Quicken too much work (as the founder of Mint.com did, apparently). If you find even this application too challenging, you might try Rudder (www.rudder.com).

Online Banking

If you are truly into the Web 2.0 thing (Facebook, Twitter, MySpace, etc.), you will—or already do—appreciate the simplicity of online banking. By paying bills online, by getting your paycheck deposited directly into your bank account, and with committed use of your debit card, you may never have to look at a piece of paper from your bank again. *Forbes Magazine* reported that one fourth of all adults are online banking customers, and they even rated the online banking services of all the major financial institutions, ranking Citicorp, Bank of America, and Wells Fargo, along with several Internet-only banks as their "Best of the Web" picks.[3]

Online Bill Paying Versus Writing Checks

Most of us write a lot fewer checks these days with the proliferation of debit cards and the notoriously extensive use of credit cards by American shoppers. But still there are the monthly bills from the electric company, the phone company, and the rent or mortgage payment.

---

1. *PC Magazine* online review by Kathy Yakal, posted April 3, 2009, and updated April 28, 2009.

2. http://www.mint.com/about/

3. http://www.forbes.com/bow/b2c/category.jhtml?id=3

If you're fairly computer savvy, you may already be paying these bills online as well, although I suspect most of us still write checks for them, as I do (maybe that's why I suspect that you still do). My excuse is I'm too set in my ways to develop a new habit. It's hard to find a more substantive excuse than that, because once set up, online bill paying has some distinct advantages that you might want to consider if you aren't too set in your ways:

- No checkbook to carry around with you (or misplace)
- No envelopes to lick or stamps to buy
- No worries about the post office losing your payment and costing you late fees or a telephone negotiation with your creditor
- Scheduling your payment for days ahead and going on your way worry free, knowing the money will get there on time

Of course if you worry, as I do, that one day the Internet will be down just at the very moment you have to get online, these modest benefits may not sway you, this despite protests from my tech-savvy friends that this really can't happen anymore except for brief moments. You may instead counter with the following:

- Remember that one time your bank didn't get it right, and all your bills were late that month (that's the month I moved back to paper—it was over 5 years ago, but I haven't forgotten).
- You don't have to find a computer and log in to look up a single payment you made last month; it's right there on your check stub, if you remembered to enter it and haven't misplaced it, of course.
- When you have it on paper in your pocket, you have confidence that no one can take away from you, not a power failure, a hard disk crash, or a would-be Internet-based identity thief—hard to argue with this one.

Tracking Balances, Transferring Funds, and Other Fun Stuff

The last of my nice-features-of-online-banking pitch is the ability to

- easily know what your bank thinks your balance is—it's good for you to know that, even though they don't yet know about checks you've written that haven't reached them.
- move money from one account to another—savings to checking or vice versa—within a minute or so at the kitchen table

instead of waiting for the mail delivery or making a trip to the bank or placing a 10-minute phone call and wading through all the voice mail screening.

Final Thoughts About Online Banking. The bottom line in online banking—break an old habit and try it. The positives really do outweigh the negatives. Managing your money should be made as easy and require as little time as possible, since you've already spent a fair amount of effort earning it. Banks are working hard to get us to stop going into the branch so much, and that is to our benefit as well as theirs.

Protecting Yourself From Identity Theft

All this talk about doing your banking online—writing checks using information stored on your computer, giving passwords to computers in places you'll probably never see—can't really wrap up without a few words about identity theft. Consumer's Union, publisher of *Consumer Reports,* tells us that there are more than 8 million new victims of identity theft each year in the United States. It's not that all identity theft occurs through the use of technology or even that most of it does. It's just that with a far-flung computer network, we can't see what's happening to our data, and what we can't see, we tend to worry about.

According to the Federal Trade Commission (FTC), identity theft can take a variety of forms, such as the following:

1. *Dumpster Diving.* They rummage through trash looking for bills or other paper with your personal information on it.

2. *Skimming.* They steal credit or debit card numbers by using a special storage device when processing your card.

3. *Phishing.* They pretend to be financial institutions or companies and send spam or pop-up messages to get you to reveal your personal information.

4. *Changing Your Address.* They divert your billing statements to another location by completing a change-of-address form.

5. *Old-Fashioned Stealing.* They steal wallets and purses, mail (including bank and credit card statements), preapproved credit offers, new checks or tax information, and personnel records or even bribe employees who have access to your information.

6. *Pretexting.* They use false pretenses to obtain your personal information from financial institutions, telephone companies, and other sources.[4]

As you can see, not all of these come from using technology. Some of them come from just ordinary living, like changing your address when you move, carrying a purse, or using a credit card when you visit a restaurant. Truly the best identity theft protection is diligence in protecting and sharing elements of your identity with others.

So here are some (hopefully) comforting tips, again from the FTC's website:

- *Protect your Social Security number.* Don't carry your Social Security card in your wallet or write your Social Security number on a check. Give your Social Security number only when absolutely necessary, and ask to use other types of identifiers.
- *Treat your trash and mail carefully.* To thwart an identity thief who may pick through your trash or recycling bins to capture your personal information, always shred your charge receipts, copies of credit applications, insurance forms, physician statements, checks and bank statements, expired charge cards that you're discarding, and credit offers you get in the mail. Shredders are widely available at modest cost.
- *Be on guard when using the Internet.* There are so many ways to use the Internet and just as many ways thieves can get to your information. The FTC has actually set up an online site at www.onguardonline.gov devoted to giving you lots of information about this subject.
- *Select intricate passwords.* Use passwords on your online credit card, bank, and phone accounts. For most sites, this will be required. Avoid using easily available information like your mother's maiden name, your birth date, the last four digits of your Social Security number or your phone number, a series of consecutive numbers, or a single word that would appear in a dictionary. Of course, remembering all those passwords can be a challenge, and for that I recommend RoboForm,[5] a very low-cost program that will manage all your passwords for you,

---

4. http://www.ftc.gov/bcp/edu/microsites/idtheft/consumers/about-identity-theft.html

5. http://www.roboform.com/

keep them encrypted, and automatically fill in password fields on your command.

- *Verify sources before sharing information.* Don't give out personal information on the phone, through the mail, or on the Internet unless you've initiated the contact and are sure you know who you're dealing with. Identity thieves are clever and may pose as representatives of banks, Internet service providers (ISPs), and even government agencies to get people to reveal their Social Security numbers, mother's maiden name, account numbers, and other identifying information.

- *Safeguard your purse and wallet.* Protect your purse and wallet at all times. Don't carry your Social Security number or card; leave it in a secure place. Carry only the identification information and the credit and debit cards that you'll actually need when you go out.

- *Store information in secure locations.* Keep your personal information in a secure place at home, especially if you have roommates, employ outside help, or are having work done in your house. Share your personal information only with those family members who have a legitimate need for it. Keep your purse or wallet in a safe place at work; do the same with copies of administrative forms that have your sensitive personal information.

As I look over this list, I can't help being dismayed by the efforts we have to go to today to avoid having someone steal from us. The conveniences of modern life come with a price, to be sure, unlike the simpler lives our parents and grandparents enjoyed. Of course you could simply revert to the ways they conducted their affairs—no credit cards, no computers—and carry your money in your underwear (OK, I made that one up). But do you really want to surrender the conveniences to avoid the risks?

Credit freeze is one more defense for those who choose to live in today. Did you know you can keep others from accessing your credit report? One defense against identity theft would be to prevent a thief from opening an account in your name, and a good way to do that would be to prevent the would-be creditor from accessing your credit report in order to approve the credit. You can do that by simply applying to the state where you reside for a credit freeze. There are some modest fees to pay in some states, and a legitimate creditor would have to get your permission to lift the freeze for them to access it, so there is some effort you might have to expend when applying for credit yourself, but the security would be pretty good.

Many identity theft victims find that crooks have used stolen personal information like Social Security numbers to open new accounts in their victims' names. When a credit freeze is in place at all three major credit bureaus,[6] an identity thief cannot open a new account, because the potential creditor will not be able to check the credit file. When you are legitimately applying for credit, by contrast, you can lift the freeze temporarily using a personal identification number (PIN) so legitimate applications for credit or services can be processed. You can read lots more about this and find out the rules in your state by visiting www.consumersunion.org/campaigns/learn_more/003484 indiv.html.

SUMMARY OF KEY IDEAS FOR CHAPTER 13

1. Whatever personal computer you choose, get lots of memory and storage capacity. Their low cost and capacity to extend the usability of your computer make shortchanging them to save a few dollars a really bad decision.

2. For bookkeeping software you keep on your computer, Quicken by Intuit is hard to beat. If you are considering another maker, compare features to Quicken before you buy.

3. If you're comfortable with keeping your data on the Internet—which is to say on someone else's computer—online bookkeeping software is becoming very capable and user friendly.

4. Online banking and bill paying are very easy to use these days and available from virtually all banks. Avoiding check writing alone has been enough to convert some users.

5. Identity theft isn't something that always happens to the other guy, and you don't have to be cruising the Internet to be vulnerable. If you value your assets and your reputation, take reasonable precautions with all your personal information.

---

6. http://www.equifax.com, http://www.experian.com, and http://www.transunion.com

14

Retirement Planning

So You Can Live Well for 100 Years

There are lots of words written these days about postponed retirement, nonretirement, working until you drop, and so on. While retirement circumstances have certainly changed over the past couple of years, much of the hype is just that—media-induced fear. If you are in the early years of your career, your ability to retire and enjoy your retirement is still intact (unless you planned to retire in the next few years, in which case, the following checklist should be helpful). What has changed is the importance of planning for it sooner rather than later. All the experts have said that for years, of course, and we all nodded our heads and then went on about our business as if nothing had been said and nothing had changed.

Well, it is different now, if for no other reason than that we have seen firsthand how quickly casually made investments can turn down and taken-for-granted home values can be lowered at a rate not seen since the Great Depression. The thing to keep in mind is this: That condition is not permanent—it exists today because of the events of the past few years, and it will correct itself over time as it always has, although perhaps not as quickly as we would like. Values that existed immediately before the Great Depression would represent phenomenal values today, even after the collapse of values in the ensuing years, except of course for bets on speculative investments that should never have been made in the first place. So if you've followed the advice I've offered you in earlier chapters, you have a sound investment program, a good, affordable home, and a sensible process for handling your daily finances. Now it's time to start thinking about the time when you'll not need or want to work any longer.

A Checklist for Those in Midcareer

If your retirement fund was severely bitten by the meltdown in the financial markets and you have less than 10 years before your planned retirement, you have a time problem—there may not be enough time for your investments to recover before you start drawing on them. Here are the seven best ideas I could find for helping you to make up that difference:

1. *Delay your retirement a few years.* An obvious choice, this has the dual advantage of adding to your retirement fund and shortening the number of years you will need to rely on those funds for support.

2. *Postpone filing for Social Security.* As you'll see, waiting to file will increase the amount of your monthly benefits, and if you live a long life, it will increase the total amount of benefits you ultimately receive.

3. *Avoid early withdrawals.* Taking money out of your retirement fund to support spending decisions while you are working is almost always a bad move. The only exceptions would have to be critical health issues that can't be avoided or funded any other way.

4. *Take a hard look at your risk tolerance.* It's unreasonable to think you can make up the losses by taking greater risks with the money you have left. For most of us, that simply exposes us to even more losses the next time the market dips.

5. *Rebalance your portfolio.* If your investment portfolio was 50% in stocks before the decline, it's certainly below that today. Whatever rebalancing means to you, you should probably be adding equity stocks back into your portfolio now.

6. *Refinance your mortgage.* A 1% drop in interest can save you hundreds of dollars a month. With today's historically low interest rates, you'll not likely find a better time to refinance your mortgage, assuming you can find your way through the

nervous patchwork of new rules banks have set up to protect themselves from more bad loans.

7. *Increase your retirement fund contributions.* This may hurt your current living standards a bit, but that may be a small price to pay to avoid a lower standard of living for the rest of your life after your income has stopped.

Financial planners (see the later discussion) and investment advisers often quote statistics that show that we are living longer than ever before, and so we will need more retirement income to support us during all those additional years on the planet. There are also charts that show we are retiring sooner than ever before and imply a direct relationship between early retirement and long life, further reinforcing the case for more saving and retirement planning. Whether that's statistically true or not, I do not believe the relationship is a direct one—it just looks that way because no one has measured the relative life expectancy of those who completely retire compared to those who move from committed, full-time work to service that gives them pleasure and benefits others, such as volunteer work.

In either case, it's pretty clear that we are living longer than our parents and will need food and fun money while we're here. I recently read that a child born today can expect to live to age 100, assuming current trends continue. So be sure to buy a copy of this book for your children, too, and give it to them the day they start shopping for college and begin planning their lives and work. But for now, for today, this book is for you. So let's see what you need to do today to get ready.

Assessing Your Postretirement Needs

How much will you need to live on during your post-full-time-work years? That's the first question to ask yourself, whether you will be fully retired or not. Then you have to ask how long you will need it— that is, how long you will live in retirement. Assuming you have or plan to have a family, that refers to both you and your spouse, likely to be the only family members left at home by then. The sequential process might work something like this:

- Determine how much money you will need each year in retirement for living expenses, travel, health care, and so forth.
- Determine how many years you plan to live, considering current mortality tables, and how you think your lifestyle might

make your experience different (I used a calculator at msn.com[1] that said I'd make it to 102—yikes).

- Look at your current savings rate, IRAs, 401(k)s, and the like, and project what that will all build to by the time you retire, forming the foundation for your retirement fund.
- Add Social Security[2] and other pension benefits you expect to be entitled to by then, considering your age at retirement, any income that might reduce your benefits, and so on.
- Calculate the probable earnings of income-producing assets you will have by then and the rate at which they will be depleted.
- Consider the gradual conversion of unneeded assets into cash, including your house, and those whose earning power will no longer be adequate, requiring you to sell the asset and use the proceeds to live on.
- Use present-value calculations to determine if your income will pay your expenses for as long as you and your spouse are alive.

Simple, huh? Well, at least the logic makes sense, but the calculations usually require pretty extensive electronic spreadsheet models with fancy formulas and lots of assumptions about how long things will last, what your investments will earn 10 or 20 years from now, and so on. You may be able to find a scaled-down version of such a model in your bookkeeping software.

So let's just look at the first step, a necessary starting point and something you can reasonably estimate and will need regardless of where you go for help. What will you need or want to spend in your retirement years? To get a handle on this, dig out your checkbook for the past 12 months, and start making a list. The list will have on it all the things you think you'll still need to spend for by then along with amounts per year. Now, keep in mind that you'll not be working every day, so your commuting expenses will go way down, your need for work clothes will pretty much disappear unless you have a garden, health insurance will be largely replaced by Medicare and a good supplemental policy, and with luck, your mortgage and other debts will be paid off by then. Payroll taxes will go away too. Payments for term life insurance will probably go away by then, although whole life premiums may continue.

On the flip side, you'll have more leisure time, so travel might see a big increase, but perhaps not with fancy hotel dinners along the

---

1. http://moneycentral.msn.com/investor/calcs/n_expect/main.asp

2. http://www.ssa.gov/planners/benefitcalculators.htm (You can use estimates here without identifying yourself.)

way. You should plan on continuing an exercise program as part of your health routine, and that might involve more green fees or tennis balls or square dancing lessons for you both. Long-term care can become a huge burden if your health declines and you've not purchased long-term care insurance in earlier years. You can find some extensive checklists and some neat calculation tools for all this at Purdue University's Extension website[3] if you're inclined to do the calculations without outside help.

When you're done, you should expect to see your total expenses decline 20% to 30% below their preretirement levels, according to most experts on the subject. If you are running your own business then instead of teaching, your expenses could decline as much as 40% to 50%, with the removal of business expenses.

The Home Mortgage Monkey

Let's suppose you're working out your plan details and the fly in the ointment seems to be the fact that you will still have some mortgage payments left to make when you reach your desired retirement age. A mortgage payment takes a big chunk out of most everyone's income, and it could easily be the difference between a rich and rewarding retirement and a monthly struggle to keep the house so you have something to fall back on or something to give to your kids. What to do?

As noted earlier in this book, by far the best option is to plan to have the house paid off before you retire. But suppose you can't do that, or suppose the payoff date will be so close to your retirement date that the money that could be going into your retirement fund is going to the bank holding your mortgage instead. Here are some ideas to consider:

1. *Give it to the kids now.* If you have children who would like to have the house when you're gone, sit down with them and see if they would be able to take over the payments today. If they can, you could grant it to them, trust it to them, or sell it to them for the remaining mortgage balance, depending on your (and their) tax situation. This relieves you of the mortgage payment, keeps you living in the house while you're still alive, and gets the house out of your estate as well (more on this in Chapter 15).

---

3. https://sharepoint.agriculture.purdue.edu/ces/retirement/toc.aspx

2. *Use the reverse mortgage option.* This is really a loan against your home in which the bank pays you every month instead of the other way around. Your loan balance builds as time goes on, to be settled by you or your estate selling the home or by your children taking over the home and repaying the loan after you're gone. In the interim, you get money to live on, either monthly or in a lump sum, instead of paying it out. The safest of these, called Home Equity Conversion Mortgages, are insured by the Federal Housing Administration up to $417,000. Conventional loans are available above that amount.

3. *Move to a retirement community; sell the house to finance the move.* This can be a rewarding option for many seniors, providing care when they need it and recreational opportunities with other seniors whenever desired. Options range from active senior communities to intensive care facilities, often on the same property. Operators commonly work out financing arrangements involving the sale of outside real estate to finance the purchase of a home inside the community grounds. Be careful here, though, as many such facilities will not give you equity you can sell or transfer to your children. When you die, the property reverts to the institution, so they can make it available—that is, sell, to another senior.

When to Sign Up for Social Security

Working Americans can choose several options when it comes to signing up for Social Security retirement income. You can choose to start collecting payments at 62 (early retirement), at 65 to 67 (full retirement age), depending on your year of birth, or as late as 69 (delayed retirement age) to get expanded benefits for waiting. Or you can pick any age in between, as benefits are prorated along the way between 62 and 69. The lowest benefits are paid to workers who select the earliest retirement age, and the highest benefits go to those who wait until age 70 to register.[4]

You can register for retirement benefits as soon as you reach early retirement eligible age, but this can be a trap. If you are still earning income in a year in which you receive early retirement benefits (before you reach full retirement age), you will have to forfeit some of

---

4. http://www.ssa.gov/OACT/quickcalc/early_late.html

the benefits that you've received. That means repaying them, usually in the form of lower benefits the following year. Since your benefits are reduced when you take an early retirement benefit, this could result in a reduced benefit that you don't even get to keep, although the Social Security Administration tells us it evens out over your lifetime. Once you reach full retirement age, you will not be required to repay any benefits regardless of how much you earn. However, keep in mind that you may have to pay income taxes on those benefits, and the more income you earn, the higher the tax bracket you'll be in. (Remember Chapter 12?)

Best solution? If you expect to live a long life, your best financial decision is to wait until age 70 before filing for benefits. If that is not financially feasible because of your overall financial situation, then simply wait as long as possible to get the highest monthly benefit you can.

Getting Help: The Financial Planner

As you get to this point in this rather complex chapter, you may be a bit overwhelmed in trying to decide how you come up with numbers that will make sense for you, numbers you can count on and plan for with some sense that you're not completely off the mark. How do you decide which options to choose, what kind of future earnings your investments can earn, what future price inflation rates may be, loan interest rates, long-term care costs, and all the rest?

Good questions. And you should be overwhelmed at trying to nail all those numbers down, because they can't be estimated with any degree of accuracy until they happen. No matter what your CPA or banker friends may tell you, no one knows. We get our answers by trying different scenarios or sets of assumptions so we can try to see the range of possibilities. Then we let our minds decide the probability of each scenario becoming the reality of the future. We financial folks call this kind of analysis "what if" analysis: What if this happens? What if that happens instead? Here are some examples:

- How will your monthly retirement income change if investment returns on stocks average only 4% going forward instead of the 11% they have averaged the past 75 years or so?
- How will your ability to travel be impacted by a 20% increase in long-term care insurance rates in the future, as insurance companies finally learn how much these policies cost them to service?

- What will be the difference in your income if you need to sell your home in a recession instead of at the top of the market?

That's why you need a financial adviser to help you. That's why you need a solid plan developed specifically for you and your family, with a variety of options played out on paper where you can see the result in black and white.

How to Choose the Right Adviser for You

The questions left to be answered: What kind of adviser should you choose, and how do you qualify him or her as the right one for you? Let's look at the choices.

Your CPA or Tax Preparer. This might seem to be a good choice because this person knows your tax situation and a lot about your income situation as well. Some CPAs offer financial planning and retirement planning services, and their industry has created the CFS (certified financial specialist) designation to indicate those who have studied the planning field. But most CPAs are not geared for this kind of service, because it's not inherent in the practice of public accounting or tax reporting, which focuses primarily on the past. Consider this source only if they can demonstrate the CFS designation *and* they've gotten additional education in the techniques needed for this service—financial forecasting, investment guidance, and the economics of real estate and the financial markets.

Your Attorney. This might be an adviser you trust, someone who knows your legal affairs and is consistently your advocate in difficult situations. With rare exception, your attorney will not be qualified to advise you on financial planning matters, and he or she will likely tell you so. The practice of law involves interpretation of the law and the legal system; it does not involve any of the skills needed for financial planning.

Your Banker. If you have a personal banker who has provided financial guidance to you in the past about your loans, your savings, and the like, you might consider this a similar kind of service. It isn't. While often well informed about the economic situation and trends in interest rates and real estate values, your banker will not be a good choice for a service that involves making projections about the future. Most bankers are trained to be risk averse, a bias that likely skews their ability to forecast your financial prospects, even if they have the analysis tools, which they typically don't.

Your Insurance Salesperson or Stockbroker. As providers of relevant services that bring you value, these folks will often represent that they can help you plan your future. The case sounds credible, because every financial plan should contain insurance and securities, and the insurance industry has even created a specialty in financial planning and a related designation, chartered financial consultant (ChFC). But these professionals earn a significant part of their compensation by making sure that your plan has insurance and securities in it, and that's a conflict of interest any way you look at it. This is not to say they are being devious with your future; it simply says they come in with a bias that may not be in your best interest, so don't take a chance.

Your Financial Planner. Huh? You don't have one of these? Well, that's probably what's missing. A financial planner is trained in a more focused area than your CPA or attorney but more broadly than your insurance or securities advisers. They are skilled in areas best suited for the kind of help you need to plan your retirement. They are trained to look at future trends mathematically, which offsets our tendencies to look at the future with some emotional attachment to how we'd like it to look. They are trained to manage the intricate spreadsheets that compare various options against the statistics of history and the expectations of the future. They will prepare your plan and (optionally) help you keep it up to date with annual or quarterly reality checks. Balanced with a healthy dose of current perspective, that is just the kind of insight you want to bring to the table now.

Validating Your Adviser's Qualifications

Now that we've identified the kind of adviser you should seek, how will you know if you've gotten one who is truly qualified to help you? Personal interviews are comforting but largely irrelevant except to establish whether you like them. Unless you plan to propose marriage, that may not be helpful. Rather, you want someone who is a scientist at designing your financial future and an artist in helping you execute the plan, someone who thinks the way you think about the choices you need to make. What might the qualification checklist look like? The website msn.com has a useful checklist of things to watch out for,[5] and the *Wall Street Journal* published a well-written checklist in April 2009.[6] Here's my list:

---

5. http://articles.moneycentral.msn.com/RetirementandWills/CreateaPlan/8Things YourFinancialPlannerWontTellYou.aspx

6. *Wall Street Journal*, April 13, 2009, "Questions to Ask When Picking an Adviser," p. R1.

1. They have earned the CFP designation awarded by the Certified Financial Planner Board of Standards Inc., the strongest overall certification in the financial planning field. There are a laundry list of other certifications that will get waved in front of you by insurance people, securities investment people, and others. They may add elements of useful expertise, but they do not replace this overall award that says the holder has studied across the entire field of financial planning. You can learn more about this designation as well as some of the others at www.cfp.net.

2. You can trust them to be honest and serve you with integrity. You have only to think of the name Bernie Madoff to know that this is important. You'll have to do some due diligence to find out if your candidate has a checkered past or a criminal record or bankruptcy following him or her or any indictments or recorded customer complaints that use words like *fraud, excessive trading,* or *arbitration awards.* A great place to check this out is www.finra.org, the Financial Industry Regulatory Authority's official website. You can't be sure, but you can be cautious, and that will protect you much of the time.

3. The primary focus of their business is financial planning. You want people who do this so much that they almost live it. They have a sense of trends and financial developments because they are constantly updating their knowledge, analyzing the headlines for what is really happening, and applying it to the advice they give their clients. Some planners are also investment advisers, offering to manage your investment portfolio for an annual fee beyond the preparation of your plan. This can be an advantage or a disadvantage to you, but it's important you keep the two services separate in your mind and in your fee negotiations (see Item 5 in this list).

4. They bring more than an Excel spreadsheet; they bring good judgment and some wisdom to the projects they take on. Talk to some of their past clients to see if they felt these traits were present. Don't engage someone who simply plugs your numbers into a spreadsheet financial model, loaded with static metrics, that produces a 50-page report you can't read.

5. Their attitude about the future makes you comfortable. That's not to say they paint a rosy picture of your millionaire retirement, but they take a generally positive attitude about the

future prospects for those who make sensible decisions along the way. If you meet someone who thinks there is very little you can do to protect yourself, and the financial system in this country is only days away from collapse, run for the door.

6. Their fees are transparent and reasonable and are solely based on the service they provide, not the products they sell. Avoid any inherent conflict of interest that may skew the advice you get, and be willing to pay for the fiduciary service you are getting. I can't tell you how much your initial plan will cost—ours cost us $2,500 a few years ago, and we considered it a small price to ensure that the advice we were getting was the only thing we were expected to pay for.

SUMMARY OF KEY IDEAS FOR CHAPTER 14

1. If we learned nothing else from the financial meltdown of 2008–2009, we've learned that sound financial planning is essential, and the sooner the better, so that we can recover from the inevitable bumps and grinds of the economy.

2. Midcareer teachers will have a bigger challenge than their younger counterparts in recovering from the decline in their investments. But some available—if not easy—choices can help them recover much of their losses and perhaps all of them.

3. Any retirement planning has to start with envisioning what your retirement years will look like. Moving from the city to a small town, touring the world, and financing the grandchildren's college fund will all require different choices.

4. If your plan says you'll have a home mortgage balance when you retire, don't despair. There are some pretty good options for getting rid of that mortgage without moving to the nearest highway underpass.

5. This is another area where you will likely need the help of a professional adviser to work through all the options. Keeping in mind that not everyone who says he or she is an expert is, this is still a great place to get help sorting out all the options objectively.

15

Wills and Trusts

Your Will: Your Last Opportunity to Have It Your Way

Making your will does not mean you are preparing to die. It means you are taking care of someone you love.

This is very good advice. You should take it. If you have no one to protect, give everything to your favorite charity—or my favorite charity. If you have a family, they need that protection today, not when you suddenly do an unplanned exit from this life. A will is exactly like a life insurance policy. You don't ever want to use it, but you will sooner or later, and that's far better than never having one to use.

Why is a will so important? Why not let the legal system sort it all out, since they're going to get involved anyway? Here are three reasons why that's a bad idea:

1. Probate—this court system oversees the orderly distribution of your estate when you die. *If you don't have a will, the state—not you—will decide who gets your assets after your final bills have been paid.* Your intentions are considered either unknown or hearsay to the court until proven.

2. Probate—*this court system will decide who manages the liquidation of your assets and who will raise your minor children.* It may be a stranger who knows neither you nor your family making those

decisions. He or she will evaluate requests from your family and decide which are honored and which are not.

3. Probate—this court system will keep your assets locked up until all decisions about distribution have been made. For a simple estate with a will, that might take 12 months. *Without a will, it can easily take several years.*

If you're getting the idea that probate is the reason you need a will, you're almost right. It's not that probate is the bad guy here. That's just the unavoidable process. Every estate must go through a probate process before the assets you own can be passed to your heirs. The probate court will determine if a valid will exists, in which case the court will try to follow the wishes outlined in the will.

But without a will to refer to, the court is left to investigate, sort out often conflicting testimony, rule on motions by anyone who challenges the authenticity of your wishes, and sometimes just guess at the right thing to do with your money. Can you imagine what that can do to the time line for distribution? Would you like your family to wait while that all works itself out, because you didn't take the time to write a will?

Getting Help With Your Estate Planning

What's involved in writing a will? First step—get some advice on how to do it. This book is *not* that legal advice; trust me on that. You will need to either hire an estate planning attorney or try to do it yourself. I strongly recommend the attorney as the way to go, but you will find many websites inviting you to take advantage of their free information that you may be tempted to use without consulting legal counsel.

Warning: Most of these sites really want to sell you something that isn't free, often including legal counsel from an attorney you'll never actually meet. Also, many of these sites offer forms for do-it-yourselfers. But like most legal rules, probate law is a state-by-state matter, and what works in one state will not work in another. Don't trust assurances from the sellers without checking it out. You may not be around to do it over if they're wrong.

In my opinion, the most credible of these, and probably the longest in the business of providing legitimate legal guidance without hiring a lawyer, is www.nolo.com, an educational site that helps nonlawyers understand legal matters and handle issues that don't really require the services of an attorney. Nolo also sells do-it-yourself, make-a-will software. Their product might hold up in probate court, but again, since you won't be around to redo it if there's a snag, I recommend you make sure it's done right the first time.

OK, now that you've got help, what do you ask for? There is more to thorough estate planning than just a will, although that is the cornerstone of your plan. A good estate planning attorney will have his or her own checklist, as ours did. Here's my suggested starting list, based on our experience (life partners with no minor children):

- Your last will and testament—your final statement of intentions regarding your estate, which assets go to which heirs, who gets whatever is left, what penalties will be levied for contesting the will, and who you choose as executor(s) to manage the process and make the decisions
- Health care directive—the document that you use to indicate how you want to be cared for medically in your final days—including any limits on life-extension measures for terminal conditions—in the event you aren't able to say so for yourself at the time
- Power of attorney (POA)—giving another person the right to make legal decisions involving the management of your property if you are alive but unable to make them for yourself (There are a variety of these, so ask about the options in your state.)
- Any trust agreements that you and your attorney choose to help you pass selected assets to heirs before you die, to gift money or property to charities, or to remove them from your taxable estate (These too will vary by state and purpose.)

What You Can Do Ahead of Time

Aside from having an up-to-date will, you can use several techniques and tools to minimize the impact on your family of having to deal with your death and the frozen finances during the probate process. Here are some ways to keep assets out of the probate process entirely:

1. Probate deals with assets you alone own, not those owned by you and someone else jointly. So any asset you hold in joint tenancy[1] with your spouse, for example, will automatically be owned by your spouse when you die, no probate required. Your home and other investment real estate come to mind as first choices.

2. Assets that have a defined beneficiary will automatically pass to that beneficiary upon your death. Think insurance policies,

---

1. Joint tenancy with right of survivorship (JTWROS) is the official label for this form of ownership. It means both of you own the asset together, and neither of you owns any part of the asset separately and distinctly from the other person.

securities accounts, certificates of deposit, and anything to which you have designated a beneficiary. Ask your banker about payable-on-death registration for your checking and savings accounts.

3. Assets placed in certain kinds of trusts will usually effectively remove them from your estate and convey the assets in the trust to its beneficiaries upon your death. Trusts have many ways to benefit you and your beneficiaries while you are alive as well as afterward. Keep reading to learn more about trusts and how they can help you save taxes and support your future plans.

4. Giving assets to your children during your lifetime will remove them from your estate as long as the gift occurs more than three years before your death. This also has the benefit of saving income taxes and, when done right, gift taxes as well. I have a retired client who is systematically gifting 100% ownership of her company to her children over a period of several years, all tax free (until the children dispose of it later, when they too can use estate planning techniques to pass it to their children).

5. *Planned giving* is granting to a nonprofit organization the right to own an asset, either now or after your death, but preserving your use of the asset or the income from that asset or both while you're alive. You might, for example, want to retain the dividends from your stock portfolio while you're living but want the charity to have the stock after you're gone. This technique enables a charity to either anticipate your gift or receive it immediately, gives you immediate tax benefits, and generally removes one more asset from your estate for probate and estate tax purposes.

Some Closing Thoughts About Wills

1. I really want you to think about this one: Do you have a charitable cause that you value but have not been able to support to the extent you would like because you didn't feel you could afford it? Your last wishes become the place where you can take care of that. Why this pitch when you've already paid for the book? Charities suffer more than most of us when the economy takes a hit for a couple of reasons. They really want to continue to help everyone they have been helping, and usually there are even more people that need help during difficult times. But at the same time, their traditional sources of income tend to dry up during these same periods. Governments cut back on contracts for services because their tax revenues have fallen, and wealthy

foundations cut back on gifts because their sources of wealth, typically stock market and real estate values, have taken a hit too. Your gift to your charity at a time when you no longer need the money can be a life-sustaining blessing at just the right time. *And* if your gift comes out of your trust or is a planned-giving gift, its value escapes the probate court and likely provides favorable tax benefits as well. In the end, however, if your family needs every dollar you can give them, this may not be for you. But it's something to discuss with your adviser.

2. On the flip side, we've all heard of messy court fights when a celebrity or wealthy individual dies and various heirs begin battling over who gets what, trying to overturn provisions in the will that don't favor them—think Howard Hughes, Anna Nicole Smith, or Michael Jackson. It doesn't happen only to celebrities, even though they're the only ones who get the press coverage. Assuming you think you did the right thing when you made your will, and you'd like the family to accept it, you'll need to insert a provision that says anyone who contests the will shall not inherit anything from it. That deterrent to dispute is a stock paragraph that estate planning attorneys know about, but it's important that you know about it too, just in case you were to overlook my suggestion that you engage an estate planning specialist for this purpose.

3. Assets that cannot be transferred by a will alone include these:[2]
   a. Property titled in a revocable trust
   b. Property titled in joint tenancy
   c. Retirement accounts
   d. Life insurance
   e. Annuities
   f. Pay-on-death bank accounts and brokerage accounts

4. You will need to choose an *executor*, someone to manage the process of executing the requirements in your will. You will often want to choose someone you trust to be honest and fair, always a good idea. But suppose that person knows nothing about assets, stocks, real estate, or the other things you've accumulated or has little time to devote to the job. Some people may even have trouble managing their own money, but they're honest and they care. Choose a coexecutor to support the executor—a knowledgeable individual or even your bank's

---

2. *Legacy: Conversations About Wealth Transfer,* Northern Trust Corporation, 2008, p. 46–47.

trust department. They can do the job together. Alternatively, your will may give your trusted executor the authority to hire the support he or she needs and pay for it with estate money.

Trusts: Making Decisions Now That Provide Long-Term Benefits

A trust is an agreement between an owner of an asset (you, an individual) and a trustee (most anyone, perhaps a bank, perhaps you as trustee) under which the trustee will take control of the asset in order to carry out your instructions as spelled out in the trust agreement for the benefit of a beneficiary (a spouse or a child or a charity, for example). Despite the perception that trusts are for the wealthy, they are available to anyone at modest cost, and they can bring significant benefits in a number of areas:

- Enabling the management of your assets if you become unable to manage them yourself
- Making a donation to a charity when you want to attach certain conditions to the gift
- Reducing the size of your estate for tax and probate purposes
- Facilitating the tax-advantaged transfer of assets to your heirs
- Preserving your accumulated wealth for future generations
- Protecting your assets from creditors, should your financial affairs dictate the need

Living Trusts: Controlling Assets Without Owning Them or Giving Them Away

Living trusts were first used in 16th century England. Kings wanting to limit land ownership oversaw redistribution of property when a landowner died (a form of probate). To avoid disclosure of their landholdings, people set up trusts with the church to bypass the king. Landowners deeded property to their church in exchange for the promise that the church would grant the land back to their heirs when the landowner died.[3]

There are more versions of trust arrangements than I could cover in this book even if I knew them all, which I don't. Let me instead describe for you what my partner and I did with our estate planning

---

3. http://www.livingtrustvswill.com/what-is-a-living-trust.php

and why, and perhaps that will give you a frame of reference for what you might want to do.

We had been together for 18 years when we finally decided it was time to revise our wills and put everything in order for the rest of our lives. (Notice we loafed around about this for a few years before we took action—lesson learned from our parents: *Do as I say, not as I do.*)

We had our wills updated; we drew up our medical directives and our POA agreements. When we inquired about taxes and probate, our attorney brought up the idea of a revocable living trust. Our objectives were several:

1. To provide for my wife if anything should happen to me and to have it handled without a lot of hassle at that particular time in her life

2. To avoid probate court in the states where we own property (two states as this is written) and the delays in distribution that probate carries with it

3. To remove as much of our collective estates from estate taxation as possible (just in case we should build an estate large enough to get past whatever the federal estate tax exclusion would be at that time)

4. To not lose operating control of any of our assets while we are alive

What does the living trust do for us that our wills couldn't? The most obvious benefits are avoidance of probate and estate tax, but it also allows us to plan for the possibility of being incapacitated before we die. It allows us to keep our financial affairs out of the public record, since trusts are private documents. We can exercise some control over the assets we are distributing to others in ways that are not possible with a will, which mostly controls who gets the asset, not how they can use it. By the way, since we are the trustees of our trust, we have full control over what the trust does with everything during our lives, because the trust is us, in a way. Our attorney even drew up for us an agreement that (supposedly) automatically puts into our trust anything we forgot to transfer in the event we die before doing it. I sure hope that works.

We discovered one drawback recently while refinancing our home mortgage. Most banks will not accept real estate as collateral if it is held by a trust. They will require that the property be taken out of the trust so they can perfect their lien. After recording the lien, the borrower is free to put the property back into the trust. It's a nuisance if you refinance frequently, for sure. But again, it's worth the effort in my view, for the protection.

While we don't have young children at home, other living trust advantages that you might find helpful are the ability to dictate when your children are entitled to take possession of your assets—for example, upon reaching a certain age. Also if any of your heirs have special needs, controlling how they or their guardians can use the assets they are inheriting may be valuable. A will dictates who gets what, and then its job is done, while a living trust can continue into existence and be adhered to throughout the entire lives of your beneficiaries.

We would not have thought of those things without the help of our estate planning attorney. The modest additional cost to set up our trust seems well worth it.

SUMMARY OF KEY IDEAS FOR CHAPTER 15

1. The cold, hard facts: If you die without leaving behind a valid will, your heirs could wait months or even years before they are able to take possession of whatever assets you've left them, even if they're broke.

2. The probate court system is the tool used by our legal system to ascertain that your estate is being properly handled. But without careful planning, this good purpose can go seriously awry.

3. Your estate planning should include not only a will but also a health care directive, appropriate POA authorizations, and probably at least one trust agreement to minimize the delays in distributing your assets.

4. You can effectively and legally remove assets from your estate in various ways, thus ensuring they go to your heirs immediately and without estate tax liability. You should explore these options and use as many of them as make sense to you and your family.

5. A living trust may be the most useful of all forms of trusts for people of moderate means. These relatively inexpensive legal tools enable you to avoid the probate process, provide for your possible disability before you die, keep your financial affairs private, and more.

16

Final Thoughts

We've covered a huge amount of information in the pages of this book. Yet in much of the book, we've only scratched the surface of what you would need to know to be fully conversant in that area. For example, the chapters on investing in stocks, bonds, and real estate could have covered volumes all by themselves. I've spent years learning how to invest more successfully—and I'm still learning. The chapters on retirement planning, wills, and trusts are also addressing the topic from 30,000 feet. Some people spend their entire careers learning the fine points of those specialized topics.

My purpose here was not to make you an expert on any of these subjects—despite the veiled hint of that in the book's title. Rather, I wanted to help you get enough familiarity with each topic to remove the discomfort and uncertainty that comes with knowing very little about something that's important to you. The ultimate objective, of course, is to encourage you to live your financial life in a sound, responsible way and have a good life in the process. To me, that's financial mastery.

I hope you'll consider this book a reference book rather than a textbook that gets stored in the garage after the class is over. While I didn't try to provide all the answers, reading over the chapter on mortgages before you go shopping for a loan or the chapters on securities investing before you decide on your investment policy or even the section on credit cards before you accept that mail offer should provide important tips for success. And that's the point.

So here are highlights to refresh you on the best way to use what you've learned:

- The summary at the end of each chapter outlines the most important points covered. You should be able to read any of those lists and be familiar with what each point means. If you're not, go back and reread that section.
- If several of the summary points are still unfamiliar to you, it's probably a good idea to reread the entire chapter again. None of the summary points is irrelevant; when you're planning your estate protection strategies, it's not safe to gloss over one or two of the key points, even if you understand the rest.
- Every good reference book should present the opportunity to contact the author with specific questions. This one provides that opportunity as well. Specific questions can be addressed to me at Gene@GeneSiciliano.com, as long as you give me a little time to respond.

A rich, rewarding, happy, and successful life is not a function of your income. It's a function of your state of mind. We choose to be happy with what we have created, or we choose to be unhappy with what has been created for us. The difference is our attitudes about it. This book is simply intended to give you more reasons to be happy, more reasons to feel successful, more reasons to love the wonderful profession of teaching and to be joyful at the prospect of making it your life's work. I admire you and everything you do for our children. Please keep doing it.

Index

CORWIN

A SAGE Company

The Corwin logo—a raven striding across an open book—represents the union of courage and learning. Corwin is committed to improving education for all learners by publishing books and other professional development resources for those serving the field of PreK–12 education. By providing practical, hands-on materials, Corwin continues to carry out the promise of its motto: **"Helping Educators Do Their Work Better."**

In compliance with GPSR, should you have any concerns about the safety of this product, please advise: International Associates Auditing & Certification Limited The Black Church, St Mary's Place, Dublin 7, D07 P4AX Ireland EUAR@ie.ia-net.com